KV-374-483

Prehistoric Animals

by Vernon Mills

Illustrated by Vernon Mills, Frances Vargo,
Andrew Farmer and Janet Smith

Foreword by Maurice Wilson

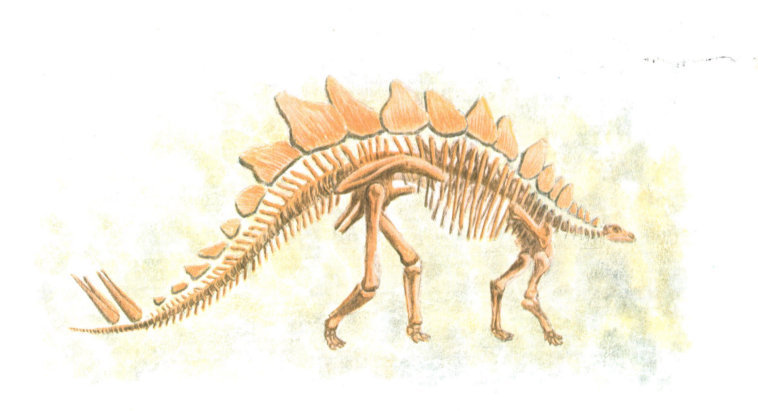

PURNELL

Foreword

by Maurice Wilson

The story of life before history is endlessly fascinating. It covers many millions of years, from enormously distant early times when there were only watery creepy-crawlies (some much like creatures alive today and others of species that have utterly vanished) until the time when man arrived to dominate and, like any other over-crowded animal, foul his surroundings.

In this book Vernon Mills, while referring to preceding times, concentrates on what has been called the Age of Reptiles. During this time a succession of reptiles appeared, developed, and branched out into many habitats and ways of living. Some took to the sea and became superficially fish-like, much as our present-day whales have done. Others developed long fingers, from which a web was stretched to form a wing like that of a modern bat. But most fascinating of all, there were the huge, fantastic dinosaurs whose remains are today the most spectacular fossils in our great museums.

Inhabiting the earth at the same time as these monsters were small, obscure mammals, and during the latter part of the Age of Reptiles there were also birds in great variety. Unfortunately, owing to the fragility of their bones, we have few remains of these.

Prehistoric Animals

© 1970 Purnell & Sons Ltd.
Published by Purnell Books,
Berkshire House, Queen Street,
Maidenhead, Berkshire
Reprinted 1971, 1973, 1974, 1976
SBN 361 01540 2
Printed by Purnell & Sons Ltd,
Paulton (Avon) and London

Contents

GEOLOGICAL PERIODS: LANDSCAPE, CLIMATE ß DEVELOPMENT

Devonian 400 Million years ago	Carboniferous 350	Permian 270	Triassic 225	Jurassic 180
Warm; mountain building, land increases	Warm, moist; thick forest	Cooler; deserts lakes and volcanoes	Hot, dry, warm sea	Warm seas spread; swamps and rivers

Above: This chart shows the periods covered by the book with some of their typical plants and animals, climate and geography. Right: The skeleton and outline of Brontosaurus compared with the silhouette of a six foot man.

Introduction

A backward leap in time

IF WE want to think about prehistoric animals, we have got to make a huge and imaginative backward leap in time. Most of us can imagine what it was like to live in our Grandfather's time, before the invention of television or jet engines. We can go and see all the things that were used in those times and even hear from some very old people what it was like to live, say in 1900. In history books we can step further back and study life hundreds or thousands of years ago. There is still plenty of evidence of how people lived in Egyptian times, for instance. If we go to the south of France, or parts of South Africa, we can see cave paintings made by some of our ancestors twenty thousand years ago.

All these periods we have considered existed when the earth was already formed. The vast oceans and seas and continents were much as they are today. When we talk of changes that took place, we think in terms of a few hundred years. In looking at prehistoric animals we shall start four hundred million

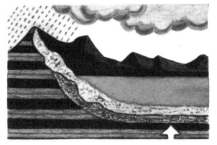

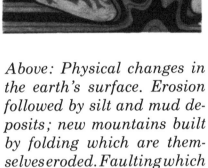
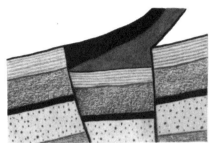

Above: Physical changes in the earth's surface. Erosion followed by silt and mud deposits; new mountains built by folding which are themselves eroded. Faulting which changes the relative level of strata; volcanic eruption producing lava and ash deposits.

years ago – an almost impossible length of time to imagine!

We shall look at changes that took millions of years, at animals that thrived on this earth for sixty or seventy million years. We shall start at a time when the oldest of our mountains were being formed; when the earth's surface was gradually becoming green through the growth of plants and trees. The climate over a great part of the earth was warm and mostly dry, except for periodic deluges of rain.

At this time the area covered by sea and shallow water was vast. Many land areas that were later to appear were being created by the washing down of sand, mud and pebbles, and by the movements of the earth's surface. In the far off time we are going to consider, the surface of the earth was changing. Not only through erosion (wearing away by rain and sea water and wind) but by volcanic activity. Huge areas of land mass were heaved up and crumpled, so that what had been sea bed was pushed up to become dry land. Existing land masses sank to become vast shallow lakes and seas. Altogether an exciting and rather terrifying prospect.

These great periods of change are so long that we don't talk in terms of a particular year, or even a century. We use geological periods of time, forty, fifty, even eighty million years long. These periods, Jurassic, Cretaceous and so on, refer to when certain types of rock were being formed. Since the

Above: Typical Devonian sea shore, with a lobe-finned fish crawling on to the land to go in search of deeper water.

remains of the animals, or evidence of their existence appears in the layers of rock, it is simplest to relate the animals to the geological period. To help you I have drawn a chart of these periods with their approximate dates and their main characteristics. You will find it on page 10.

Apart from the time factor we have another problem in this book – names. Prehistoric animals have very difficult names. All our knowledge of these animals has come from the discoveries of scientists over the past hundred years. Now, scientists like to have things clearly labelled so that there is no confusion or misunderstanding. Unfortunately the animals we are interested in don't have simple names like rabbit or elephant, so we shall have to manage as best we can with their rather long scientific ones. I have given the translation of some of the more interesting ones so that you can see why these animals are so called.

It's all very well to talk about things that happened so long ago, but how do we know so much about these things when there was no one to record them? They happened millions of years before man appeared on the earth. The answer to this is in the next chapter, where we shall turn detective for a time. We shall piece together the fragments of evidence, the clues to climate and geography, plant and animal life, until we have a vivid and surprisingly complete picture.

Ichthyosaur fossilisation

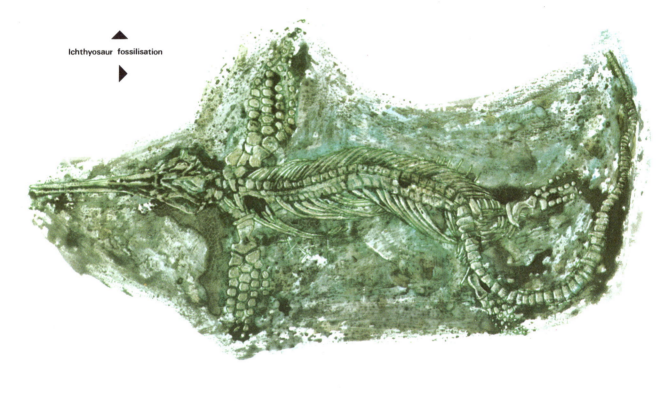

Ammonite fossil

Fossil plant

Fossil fish

The evidence in the case

EVER since the earth's crust cooled and solidified, it has been changing. Driving, lashing rain, hurricane winds and surging waters have worn away the surface. Tons of sand and mud and stones have been carried down to lower levels. Enormous pressures from inside the earth have cracked and crumpled the surface, thrusting sea beds up to become mountain ranges and drowning vast land areas. Frost and ice have shattered rocks and scoured out huge valleys.

The outer surface of the earth now consists of a series of layers we call strata, each of which was laid down at a different time in the earth's history. Each layer contains evidence of what was happening at the time, in the form of fossils. These are stone-like impressions of plants and animals. They were formed in this way; suppose an animal died and its body was washed into a stream bed. In time the carcase was covered by sand and silt, and this was squashed by further stones and mud washed down on top. Meanwhile, two things were happening. Firstly, the soft parts of the animal were rotting away, leaving the impression of their original shape in the stone that was forming from the sand and silt. Secondly, the bone and gristle were becoming saturated with water containing minerals. These minerals slowly turned the bone to something very like stone, so we call them "petrified".
Apart from this type of fossil, we have other

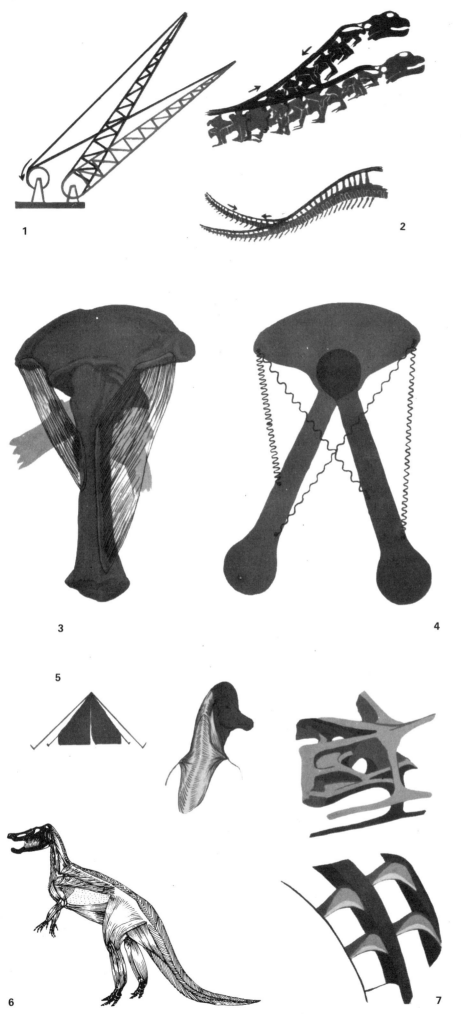

1

2

3

4

5

6

7

THE MECHANICS OF MUSCLES AND BONES: *Every animal that has a skeleton inside it is made like a piece of machinery. The muscles and tendons that join the bones together all have a particular job to do, like the parts of a simple machine.*

1. In a crane, the jib is joined to the winding drum by a cable. When this is wound in, the jib rises.

2. The long neck and tail of a dinosaur use the same system. When the muscle contracts, the head or tail are lifted.

3. The main leg bone of a dinosaur is joined to the pelvis by muscles at the front and back. They pull the leg forwards or backwards when they contract.

4. Muscles are arranged so that when one set contracts the opposite set relaxes. The hip joint is the pivot and the length of the pelvis gives the leverage.

5. Apart from joining bones together and moving them, muscles and tendons keep parts of an animal balanced. They act like guy ropes on a tent.

6. From our knowledge of animal mechanics we can reconstruct the muscles of an extinct animal. Here you see a typical dinosaur with the muscles added to the skeleton.

7. The very open vertebrae of a large dinosaur are light but strong. They are thickened only where they have to take strain or pressure. They often look very similar to modern reinforced concrete forms. The principle is the same.

Human teeth

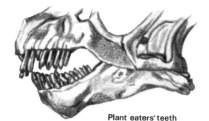

Plant eaters' teeth

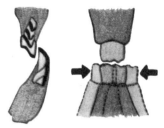

Slicing teeth   Grinding teeth

Meat eaters' teeth

Replacement teeth

Parrot beak & cheek teeth

Hypsilophodon foot

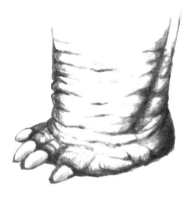

Diplodocus' foot

Tyrannosaurus' foot

evidence from animals that have died in the desert. Their carcases dried out rapidly in the hot dry conditions. This left not only the skeleton but the skin and some of the tougher parts of the insides to become fossilized. Plants, insects, fish, seaweeds and practically every other living thing was preserved in fossil form.

For millions of years this geological "treasure chest" lay undisturbed. About one hundred and thirty years ago, scientists became interested in some of the more surprising objects that had been dug up. They came to certain conclusions about these fossils by comparing them with the anatomy of present-day animals, and formed a very complete picture of what these prehistoric animals looked like, and how they lived. Let's look for a moment at how they arrived at these conclusions.

A vertebrate, that is an animal with a skeleton, must work according to a system. Its limbs and head must be connected to its body in a certain way. According to the weight they have to move, its limbs must have bones and muscles of a certain strength and thickness. After a careful examination of a complete skeleton, a scientist can "put back" the flesh that rotted away so long ago, giving us a lifelike and sometimes terrifying picture of a long-dead monster.

We can now start asking some more detailed questions. Did the animal live on land or in the water

or both? A look at its legs and feet will give us a clue; bird-like feet sink into soft mud too easily, but are very suitable for running on land. Wide heavy feet like an elephant's travel well on soft mud and may be quite effective in the water. If you look at the illustrations on page 17 you will see some of the different feet to which I have referred.

On the same page, at the top, look at the drawings of teeth. The first illustration shows a human jaw, with cutting teeth (incisors), tearing teeth (canines) and grinding teeth (molars). We have all these because we live on a mixed diet of meat and vegetables. In the other drawings you will see how the meat eaters (carnivores) had only tearing teeth. The plant eaters had mostly grinding teeth, for crushing up vegetable matter. Some animals had specially adapted teeth and jaws for snipping off shoots or cracking egg shells. We can compare paws in the same way. Some were equipped with claws for holding prey, while others were made like hands.

All these anatomical details tell us a great deal about how an animal lived. If we examine plants, insects, fish and other small creatures in the same way, we gather a great store of information. Now you can appreciate why and how we know so much about a period that no human being ever saw.

Where it all began

320 million years ago in the Devonian period

present-day
land areas

Devonian
land areas

IN ORDER to understand the animals that appeared on the earth in prehistoric times, we must look back beyond the first fossil skeletons. We have to look at a scene 375 million years ago. This period was called "Devonian" after the red rocks of Devon which were being laid down at the time.

If you look at the map on this page you will see that Europe looked very different then. Scotland and Northern Ireland were under water. England was part of a huge piece of land that covered what is now the North Sea and part of the Atlantic. A large part of what is now France and Germany was under water. The climate varied between long periods of warm dry weather and equally long periods of very heavy rain. These conditions gave rise to a very stark landscape. Volcanoes and bare mountains, great areas of sea and shallow water, and just a fringe of plants at the edge of the lakes were the dominant features.

On the land there were hardly any signs of life, but in the sea there was a teeming population of fishes and other small creatures. The fish varied in size from tiddlers to huge thirty foot monsters.

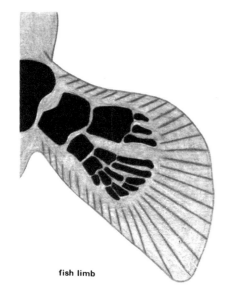

fish limb

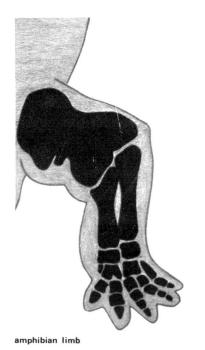

amphibian limb

There were many different forms of shell fish, together with coral formations that thrived in the warm water. The shells of these creatures were later to form a new stratum, rich in fossil information. The plants edging the water were the first to have proper roots and leaves.

Amongst the many fish in these warm seas were all the ancestors of our present-day fish. The biggest was undoubtedly *Dinichthys*, a joint-necked fish who grew to thirty feet long and lived off many of the smaller fish. He had a strong hinge connecting his bony head to the rest of his body. We still have an example of this in the rat-fish of the present day. A second group consisted of lungfish, whose developed lungs allowed them to live in the mud at the bottom of partly dried-up lakes. They too have descendants in the lungfish of today. True sharks, whose skeleton is made of gristle instead of bone, were common in these seas. Our modern sharks look very different from those Devonian ones, but basically they are very similar. The same is true of the ray-finned fish – their appearance is very different, but their structure is similar.

From fins to feet

The fish that are of particular interest to us are the lobe-finned fish. You can see a picture of one at the

jawless fish

Eusthenopteron

top of page 13. This fish is of special importance because it was he who first used his lobe-fins to crawl out of the water. Unlike most fish, *Eusthenopteron* had bones in his fins. Scientists think that when some of the shallower lakes and pools dried up in the warm season, the lobe-finned fish managed to crawl to another pool. This not only meant that they survived when others died, it also meant that over a long, long period their fins grew stronger and developed. Naturally the ones with the strongest fins had the best hope of survival, therefore only the best-adapted fish lived to have young. We shall see this situation arising time and again in the coming chapters. It is called the process of natural selection, and it is responsible for many of the changes we find in the development of an animal or a species of animal.

In the case of the lobe-finned fish it meant that over a period of millions of years, what had been a fish with fins became the first amphibian. For a long time, he kept his fish-like tail and he could only drag himself along on his rather feeble feet. He returned to the water to lay eggs and rear his young, who spent the early part of their life in the water. His name was *Ichthyostega*, and you can see what he looked like from the drawing on this page. Once on land, *Ichthyostega* grew stronger legs. His lungs

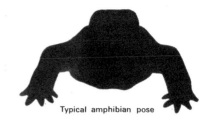

Typical amphibian pose

Development from fish to amphibian. Opposite and at bottom of page: development of bones and leg spine. Below: development of lungs. Above: typical amphibian crawling position.

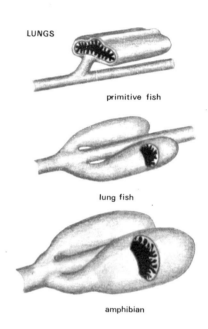

LUNGS

primitive fish

lung fish

amphibian

Ichthyostega

grew larger to give him more oxygen so that he could travel faster. He was still very dependent on the water, however, for much of his food and for breeding. It is unlikely that he stirred very far from the shores of the warm lakes and shallow seas. We know about his travels on land from the fossil footprints he left in the soft mud, and we know what he looked like from the fossil skeletons that have been found. In the next section we shall see how these amphibians developed and multiplied. The major step from fins to feet had been accomplished and the first four-legged animal had walked on the earth.

The steamy jungle: 300 million years ago

The large areas of Devonian shallow sea remained in the early part of the Carboniferous period. The millions of shell fish, sometimes forming living reefs, created layers of chalky mud when they died. This was compressed later into limestone rock. In this Lower Carboniferous rock, we find fossils of the early amphibians like *Ichthyostega* and of the rich sea life of the period.

Later, in the Upper Carboniferous period, we find a very different picture. While much of the inland area of Europe and North America was dry and desert-like, the edges of the vast continents consisted of swampy forest. The climate in these areas

Above: the formation of coal through the drowning of forests. Below: some fossil leaves, bark and stems from the Carboniferous period. At foot of page: map showing the extent of the sea in the Carboniferous period.

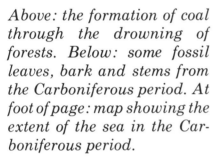

stem fossil

leaf fossil

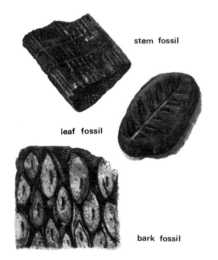

bark fossil

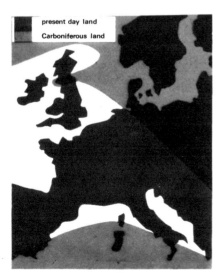

present day land

Carboniferous land

was warm and moist and this encouraged a dense tropical vegetation. The simple plants of the Devonian period had grown and developed. In the Carboniferous forest we find strange trees, up to one hundred feet high. Their trunks are patterned by the scars of the leaves that have fallen off. All the plants and trees in this forest kept their leaves all the year round, dropping them only one or two at a time. Beneath these scale trees were smaller trees with broader leaves, and then horsetails and giant ferns. Carpeting the ground was another layer largely consisting of seed ferns and true ferns. This dense undergrowth provided cover for a wide range of animals and insects. On the edge of the pools there was a variety of amphibians. Little *Miobatrachus*, only a few inches long, ran side by side with the heavy plodding five foot monster of the time, *Eryops*. In amongst the plants were all sorts of insects, mayflies, cockroaches, spiders, centipedes and scorpions. The most astonishing insect was undoubtedly *Meganeura*, a dragonfly with a thirty-inch wingspan.

The reason why the fossils of this period are so well preserved is that the earth at this time was constantly on the move. An area of land would be pushed up from under the water. Soon plants would begin to grow and then trees. In a comparatively short space of time, a dense forest was established. Then another movement of the surface would lower this piece of land, and the water would rush in and cover it. Layers of mud and the shells of sea creatures would cover the dead forest. In time it was compressed into a narrower band of peaty fibre. Millions of years later we find this layer as the hard coal we put on our fires. You can see a diagram of this on page 24, together with some of the fossils that are found in coal. In some areas this rising and falling went on for millions of years. This is why we find coal in seams, one above the other, with layers of rock in between.

The movement of the earth's surface that caused the formation of coal deposits also pushed up many of the present-day European mountain ranges. In the later, or Upper Carboniferous, period food was more plentiful and more varied. The swampy forests had provided a new environment, and the climate was warm and moist. All these factors led to changes in the types of animal that walked or swam in this tropical scene.

Different animals developed in different directions. Some of the smaller ones like *Miobatrachus* became more frog-like. Some of them returned to the water and developed a very snake-like appearance. Some of them grew large in the water and must have looked like early crocodiles, with powerful tails. One of the oddest was *Diplocaulid,* who lived on the bottom of pools and had a peculiar wedge-shaped head.

One of the most exciting developments is to be seen in the animals that spent more and more of their time on land. Some time near the end of the Carboniferous period they changed from amphibians to reptiles – that is, they gave up returning to the water to breed and lay eggs. They started to lay eggs on land!

Amphibian eggs are jelly-like and are laid in water. They do not need a shell to protect them from the sun. The water keeps them at an even temperature, and provides food for the young as soon as they hatch. When some of the amphibians developed into reptiles over a period of millions of years, they had a number of problems to solve. They had to provide

Miobatrachus

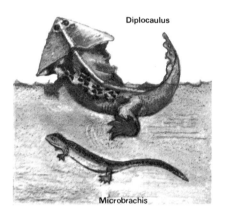

Diplocaulus

Microbrachis

Above and below: some typical amphibians of the Carboniferous swamplands. They all depended on water for their survival and breeding. It also provided their food.

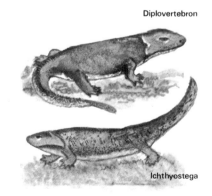

Diplovertebron

Ichthyostega

Eryops

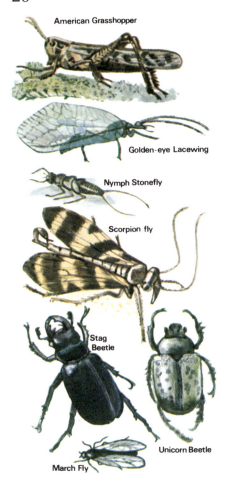

American Grasshopper

Golden-eye Lacewing

Nymph Stonefly

Scorpion fly

Stag Beetle

Unicorn Beetle

March Fly

Above: some of the insects that appeared at this time. They provided food for a number of the small amphibians. Below: the strange sail-like forms of the Pelycosaurs, both plant eating and meat eating varieties.

a suitable environment for their young, both before they hatched and immediately afterwards. This they did by laying their eggs in shells, which gave them protection from their enemies. The yolk of the egg gave the young animals an immediate source of food, and also the moist conditions it had been used to in an earlier period.

The reptiles also had to grow a tough skin, that could withstand the heat of the sun and changes in temperature. They had to develop lighter bones, stronger limbs and a more efficient heart, so that they could move faster. No longer tied to ponds and lakes, they were free to roam inland and find fresh hunting grounds.

The reptile takeover: 220 million years ago

Between the Carboniferous and the Permian periods we find a sharp change. The warm, even climate has gone. The Northern Hemisphere is cooling. Ice covers large areas of the world, even part of what are now the tropics. Great earthquakes and volcanoes are changing the face of the earth – crumpling it, folding it, heaving up great mountain ranges. The earlier seas are being divided and cut off into vast salt lakes. These changes affect all living things.

At certain times in the past the world had a climate that changed very little during the course of the

DIMETRODON

EDAPHOSAURUS

PAREIASAURUS

year. Plants and animals could be fairly sure that their conditions would not vary a great deal. They could adopt or develop a particular way of life and stick to it. For various complicated geological reasons this situation sometimes slowly changed. The climate became what we call seasonal. That is, there was a difference between the weather in, say, December and the weather in July. We take this for granted now, but it was not always so. Seasonal differences do not necessarily mean a change from hot to cold. They may mean a change from wet to dry, as they do in India in our own age.

Whatever the change, it was rarely sudden. It took millions of years and most types of animals and plants adapted to the slowly changing conditions. Seasonal differences in climate mean that plants and trees must become deciduous. That is, they must shed their leaves when the cold weather comes, and grow new ones when the sun returns. The animals that had become adjusted to temperature changes – the reptiles – had the advantage. As the swampy forests disappeared, except in isolated pockets, the amphibians diminished, and the new reptiles began to hold dominance.

Some of the Carboniferous amphibians were still around in the Permian period. There were *Eryops* and his smaller friends on the land, and strange *Diplocaulids* in the water. One of the noteworthy survivors was the big amphibian, *Mastodonsaurus*.

Above: an example of the ponderous development of the "stem reptiles". Below: the tremendous thickness of bone required to carry the heavy weight of such a monster can be judged from this drawing of his leg.

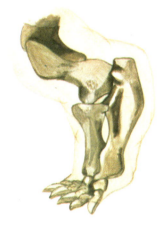

Pareiasaurus front leg structure

Captorhinus

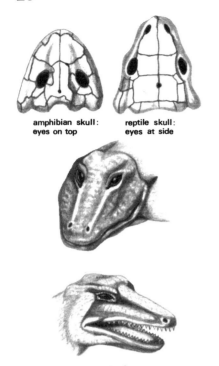

amphibian skull: eyes on top   reptile skull: eyes at side

Above: amphibian eyes set on top of head, reptile eyes on the side. Below: seasonal climate causes annular rings to form in trees.

This twelve-foot beast had a head over three feet long and a jaw full of very sharp teeth! You can see from the illustration on page 29 that he was a clumsy creature, on land at any rate. In the water he must have moved much faster, for he lived on a diet that consisted almost entirely of fish. He probably spent the greater part of his time in shallow pools where the water would keep him cool, provide his food and help to support his bulky body. Unfortunately for him, but luckily for us, the pools he lived in often dried out and he died for lack of water. He was then ideally placed for fossilization and we have some very good skeletons of him. His size and way of life did not make it easy for him to adapt to changing conditions, and he became extinct in the Triassic period.

The significant animals of this period are very different. Two sorts in particular attract our attention. The first is a group called *Eotylosaurs* (literally, stem reptiles). Some small examples of these had appeared in the Carboniferous period, but in the Permian they grew large and ponderous. You can see from the illustration of *Pareiasaurus* on page 27, just how bulky and clumsy they were. The important and exciting fact about *Pareiasaurus* was that he was the first four-footed plant eater. His peg-shaped teeth and his large stomach capacity are typical of

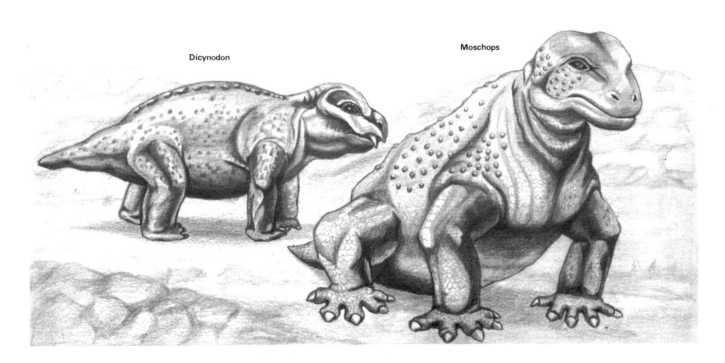

Dicynodon   Moschops

Mastodonsaurus

Above: **Mastodonsaurus**. *Below: Cutting and grinding teeth of plant-eaters. Skeleton of* **Eryops** *showing solid skull and splay feet.*

the herbivores (plant eaters). We shall find these twin elements cropping up regularly in later chapters.

At this fairly early stage of four-footed walking, the *Eotylosaurs* had not developed a very efficient skeletal mechanism. With their lower legs at a right angle to their upper leg bones, they needed very powerful muscles and thick bones to support their heavy bodies. You may find it easier to understand if you try a few press-ups!

The second group of animals that interests us, consists of the *Pelycosaurs*. Although these were quite closely related to the *Eotylosaurs*, they looked

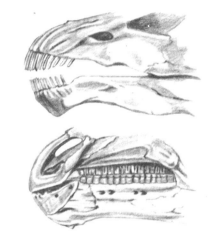

very different as you will see by a glance at the foot of page 26. The strange sail-like structure these animals had on their backs has caused a lot of comment and discussion. Most scientists now seem to agree that it was a device for controlling the body temperature. In other words, it worked like a radiator, getting rid of excess heat that would have made the animal uncomfortable; it would also have absorbed heat early in the morning to get the *Pelycosaurs* going. Cold-blooded animals like these are very reliant on temperatures outside their bodies. They have no fur or hair to insulate them, and only a relatively simple heart to pump their blood. In cold conditions reptiles become very

Volcanic eruptions and earthquakes were common in Permian times. They caused much destruction and havoc and noticeably altered the face of the earth.

sluggish and take time to "warm up" when the sun comes up. This sail device might well have given *Pelycosaurs* the edge on both their competitors for food, and their predators.

Later, these *Pelycosaurs* gave rise to a group of animals called *Therapsida* (mammal-like reptile) which included some strange creatures. *Moschops*, a slow and awkward plant-eater browsed on the edge of pools and water holes. *Dicynodont*, with two tusk-like front teeth and his jaw developed into a beak, probably shared this environment with him. Some of these animals grew to twelve or thirteen feet long with very heavy skulls. Their size and slow movement and their ungainly weight was against their survival for long, and they died out early in the next period.

Part of the pattern of this Permian period was the increase in the variety of animal life. The development of plants and animals on land provided a more varied background and diet for insects, too. We find not only an increase in their numbers, but also a number of new varieties that we know today, such as common flies, grasshoppers, lacewings and a number of different beetles. These in their turn were to provide at least part of the diet of the active young dinosaurs in the next period.

Below are shown fossils of typical sea creatures from the Permian period. From the map you can see how the land masses changed in this period.

Present-day land
Permian land

The birth of the dinosaurs

190 million years ago in the Triassic period

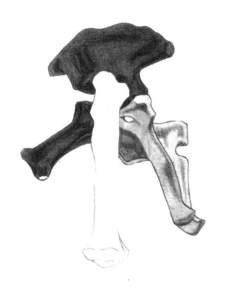

The "reptile-hip" pelvis with the pubic bone pointed forwards and downwards. We find these in the swamp dwelling plant-eaters and the meat-eaters like the one shown here, **Tyrannosaurus.**

AFTER the Permian period, when the earth had been in fairly constant uproar, the Triassic saw a return to more settled times. The world consisted mainly of two enormous continents, one in the Northern and one in the Southern Hemisphere. These were separated by a long ribbon-like sea that stretched from southern Europe through Asia to the East Indies. The continent in the Northern Hemisphere included most of what is now North America, part of the Atlantic Ocean, much of Europe and some of Russia.

Inland, these continents were largely desert and shrub-covered mountain. Here and there were salty lakes where the sea had been cut off by Permian upheavals. Large areas of what is now Britain were covered by these warm salt lakes. The climate over most of the land areas was hot and dry. Mountain-sides were covered with scree, and shifting sand-dunes were a common feature of the landscape. It is in this rather dry and scrub-covered landscape that we find the ancestors of all the dinosaurs. *Saltoposuchus* is a typical example. Several things are notable about him. Firstly, he was a *Thecodont* – that is, he had his teeth set in sockets, unlike earlier reptiles. Secondly, he walked on only two legs. His front limbs were short and didn't look very powerful. He probably used them to clutch at food, or to hold it while he was eating. He ran very well on bird-like feet, using his long tail to keep his balance, and

The "bird-hip" pelvis with the pubic bone pointed backwards and downwards. We find these in many of the plant-eaters including the armoured and horned dinosaurs. All the birds and the flying reptiles had them.

possibly as a support when at rest. A look at his teeth tells us that he was primarily a meat eater. His diet included a lot of insects and grubs. Small animals, including the newly hatched young of other animals, snails and slugs probably made up much of the rest.

Saltoposuchus was about three feet tall. He had close relatives of much the same size, such as *Procompsognathus*. It seems strange to think of these small, lightly-built creatures as the ancestors of the ungainly seventy-foot monsters of later periods. What is often forgotten is that these monsters took millions of years to reach that size and shape.

Excitement in the water

As a contrast to the small dinosaurs, another group of *Thecodonts* grew much larger. These were the *Phytosaurs*, who ranged in size from six to twenty feet. The translation of their name is interesting. It means "plant-reptile". When their remains were first discovered these animals were thought to be herbivorous. We now know that they were meat-eaters, but it is too late to change their name, so "plant-reptile" they remain.

The *Phytosaurs*, like a number of other reptiles, had returned to the water to live. Here they grew very like our modern crocodiles in appearance. For many years scientists assumed that the *Phytosaurs* were the ancestors of present-day crocodiles.

Procompsognathus

Saltoposuchus

Above: ancestors of all the dinosaurs, **Procompsognathus** *and* **Saltoposuchus**.

We now know that this is not true.

True crocodiles have a very clever arrangement which prevents them from drowning when they open their mouths under water. A double roof to their mouths allows the air from their nostrils to pass to their lungs without going through their mouths. The *Phytosaurs*, in common with some of the dinosaurs we shall meet, had a different system. In their case, the nostrils are found high up on the head, so that the air had the shortest possible route to travel to get into the windpipe. You can see from the diagram on page 35 how the two systems worked.

In spite of the title of this chapter, some of the most interesting animals in this period are the water based reptiles. The *Ichthyosaur* (literally fish-reptile) shows us just how well an animal can adapt to its environment.

As you can see from the illustration on page 35, the *Ichthyosaur* looked very like a fish. It had a streamlined body for swimming and its legs had become strong fins or paddles. Unlike most of the marine reptiles the *Ichthyosaurs* did not have to come ashore to lay their eggs. They had developed a remarkable ability. Their eggs hatched inside the mother's body and the young were born live into the water. There are fossils of the baby *Ichthyosaurs*

present-day
land areas

Triassic
land areas

ICHTHYOSAURS

inside their mother, and fossils of the babies actually emerging.

Ichthyosaurs also had a powerful swimming tail like a shark, and a fin on their backs like a dolphin. An even more fascinating feature is the strengthening ring round the eye, which probably allowed the animal to dive to great depths without the pressure damaging the delicate structure of its eye. Altogether, these adaptations to a sea life enabled the *Ichthyosaurs* to live happily through the Triassic and Jurassic periods, only to die out eventually in the Upper Cretaceous.

Also present in these Triassic seas were water-living reptiles called *Plesiosaurs*. They are often

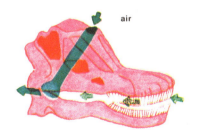

Protosuchus, *the first true crocodile, some three feet long with bony plates down his back for protection. Below: Fossils of Triassic sea creatures and, below, fossils of animal teeth – an important clue to identity.*

Protosuchus

referred to as swan-lizards because of their long flexible necks. You can get a very clear picture of what they must have looked like if you imagine a snake threaded through the body of a turtle. Unlike the *Ichthyosaurs,* they remained much more like reptiles. In fact their name means "closer to the reptile". Their legs were adapted for swimming, but at this stage were still recognizable as legs. Their bodies were flat and short like a turtle's and they swam much as a turtle does, using their limbs rather like under-water wings. Not all of them had snaky necks, but this feature gave them the chance of darting at their prey. This mostly consisted of fish and squids and other small swimming animals. Later on in the Jurassic period we shall see a remarkable development from these early *Plesiosaurs.*

Reptile hips and bird hips

Before looking at the largest dinosaur in this period, *Plateosaurus* (flat lizard), we have to understand the particular way in which scientists classify dinosaurs. Basically it is this. All dinosaurs, whatever their appearance, fall into two categories, "reptile-hip" or "bird-hip". The reptile-hips are properly called *Saurischia* and the bird-hips are *Ornithischia.* The difference is found in the bones of the hips that scientists call the pelvic girdle. These bones are a vital part of any animal, because they provide the connection between the legs and the upper part of the body. They are like the back axle in a vehicle.

The reptile-hips have a bone, called the pubic bone, which points forwards and downwards. This provides a good strong frame to which powerful muscles can be attached for moving the legs to and fro. The bird-hips have this same pubic bone, but it points downwards and backwards. They also have an extra piece of bone which points forwards and downwards. These differences are connected with an animal's ability to stand and walk on two legs.

Below: early short-necked plesiosaurs, water living reptiles with paddle-like legs adapted for swimming. They lived and developed right through the next two long periods.

Above: the phytosaurs were very like crocodiles to look at. Below: Their nostril was high on their head to keep it clear of the water.

Bipedal walking requires a very special piece of mechanics. The animal has to keep its balance as well as moving its legs, and this is a very complicated thing to achieve.

Just to confuse us, some of the bird-hip dinosaurs later went back to walking on all fours. So we cannot just say that all the two-legged dinosaurs were bird-hips and all the four-legged ones were reptile-hips. We shall have to check up as we go along. The basic differences will be clearer if you look at the diagrams on pages 32 and 33.

Most of the early dinosaurs are reptile-hips, like their ancestors. The bird-hips only became common in the next period, the Jurassic. This suggests that

millions of years of walking mostly on two legs gave rise to the adaptation of the hip joint to the more efficient bird-hip.

To return to our large dinosaur of this period, *Plateosaurus*, we find him walking on two legs in spite of his reptile-hip. He did, however, drop down on to all fours when browsing on plants, or searching for small animal life on which to feed. His back legs were noticeably stronger than his front legs – or arms – as they may more correctly be described. These arms ended in five toes or fingers, of which only one was provided with a claw. On the back leg the three inner toes had claws. *Plateosaurus* when fully developed grew to twenty feet tall.

Above: the plateosaurs who were probably the ancestors of the mighty sauropods. Below: **Plateosaurus** *walked both on two legs and four.*

Above: **Cynognathus,** *some of whose features are often found in mammals. Below: a Triassic turtle and a* **Nothosaur,** *the ancestor of* **Plesiosaurus,** *before he became aquatic.*

Not all the dinosaurs were as big as this. Towards the end of the period we find a mixture of animals. Some were light, fast-running animals of only a few feet in height. They ran leaning forwards, using their long flexible tails to balance their forward movement. Others grew to be powerful animals of twenty feet or more. Most of the smaller ones were exclusively meat eaters, but the larger ones included both gentle, passive plant eaters and powerful, predatory meat eaters. Possibly because they were trying to walk on two legs with a reptile-hip, these large Triassic dinosaurs died out in this form towards the end of the period. It is a source of great argument whether the later mighty *Sauropods* were descended from these *Plateosaurs.* Let us just say that it is likely that these, or some very similar strain, gave rise to those Jurassic monsters.

This Triassic world had other inhabitants that deserve a mention before we leave. Side by side with the *Phytosaurs,* or false crocodiles, were some true crocodiles. These were small three-foot-long reptiles, with legs and feet like modern crocodiles. They had bony plates along their back and sides for protection and were known as *Protosuchus,* that is "the first crocodiles".

Sharing much the same existence as our small crocodile were some early forms of frogs and salamanders and the earliest known turtle, *Triassochelys.* He looked very similar to our present turtles. His shell or carapace covered him entirely except for his head and tail. Unlike today's turtle, however, he couldn't tuck his head and tail inside his shell, which made him rather easier to attack. Perhaps it was some compensation to him that at that stage he still had teeth instead of the horny beak of the present turtle.

False pretences

One group of animals that give us a foretaste of the coming of the mammals are represented by the *Cynodonts* (dog-teeth). *Cynognathus* from the Lower Triassic, and *Tritylodon* from the Upper Triassic,

both have a number of features that are more usually found in mammals (that is, warm-blooded animals).

Mammal jaws have the teeth arranged in a certain order, and the jaw hinge is much simpler than in the reptiles. Both these *Cynodonts* showed these features. They also had a sort of double roof to their mouths that allowed them to eat and breathe at the same time. When this is combined with a particular sort of ribs, an animal can breathe in a rhythmical way, instead of gulping air as a reptile does.

To look at, the most noticeable change was in the position of the "knee" and "elbow" joints. These no longer stuck out as in most of the reptiles. The "knee" bent forwards and the "elbow" backwards, allowing the limbs to tuck underneath the body. This meant the animals could lie down like a dog – a new experience in the animal kingdom. There is at present not enough evidence to say whether these animals were warm-blooded or not. Nor can we be sure whether they had any fur or hair to keep them warm. It may be significant that the neck vertebrae of these animals had changed in such a way that they could have licked their fur if they had had any!

We have seen the early development of the dinosaurs. They are now ready for the major role they are to play in the next two periods. We have also seen the first glimpse of mammal-like animals. The stage is set for the great developments and excitements of the Jurassic period.

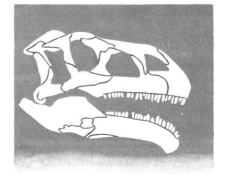

Top: **Cynognathus**, *and below* **Tritylodon,** *early mammal-like animals of the late Triassic period. Above: the skull of* **Plateosaurus**, *in which you can see the open type of construction and the leaf-shaped teeth.*

On this page you can see, above, a typical Jurassic landscape. At right, the formation of deltas which were common at this time. Far right, how and where the Jurassic deposits were laid down. Below is a world map showing in blue the vast area covered by sea at this time.

DELTA

Jurassic rock

Cretaceous rock

OXFORD

BATH

LONDON

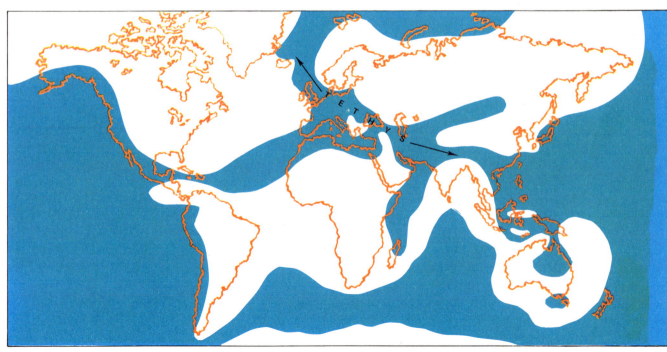

TETHYS

When the tide came in

150 million years ago in the Jurassic period

LET'S set the scene for all the exciting developments that are going to take place in the Jurassic period. The Triassic landscape was harsh. Towering mountains rose thousands of feet into the air. Their sides were constantly being broken by frost and weathering, producing stony areas called "scree". Below these stark red mountains and cliffs were vast areas of desert, and constantly shifting sand dunes with sparse scrub vegetation.

When you have large continents, the climate in the middle of the continent tends to be extreme. The sea evens out extremes of temperature, and provides a reservoir of water from which clouds may be formed. You have only to think of the relatively mild climate of the British Isles, compared with the severe climate in the centre of Russia, to see what effect surrounding seas have.

The big change from Triassic to Jurassic was closely connected with the increase of seas and shallow lakes, and the dividing up of the enormous land masses. The tall mountains of the Triassic period have been weathered and worn down, and now appear only as low hills. All the material that had been eroded from the mountains had accumulated on the plains and had silted up the rivers. There was so much of it that it even made the shallow seas muddy.

We find that most of the land areas were swampy plains and marshes, with many lakes. There were abundant forests and slow-moving and meandering rivers. The rivers threaded their way through the flat plains and emerged into the sea in wide deltas. Because of the extensive seas and the smaller land areas, there was enough rainfall for plants and trees to grow in abundance. The climate throughout the

Jurassic cycad with open and closed "flowers".

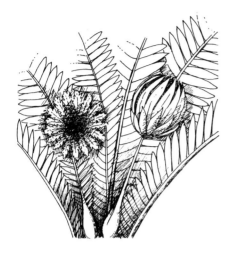

Conifer twig, seed fern and leaf of ginkgo tree.

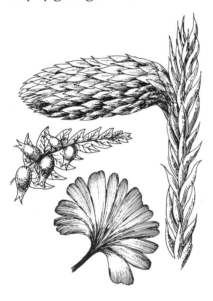

Echinoderm and ammonite. Opposite: williamsonia tree.

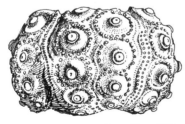

year was mild in most areas. Here and there, the trees show from their growth rings that there were seasonal differences in the weather. In some parts of the world, towards the end of the period, there were even places with a sub-tropical climate.

In common with the gentleness of the other elements, even the movements of the earth's surface consisted of slow warping. This gentle, wave-like motion constantly changed the position and depth of the shallow seas in Great Britain. The silt and sand from the mountains provided the material for what is now the area called "Oxford Clay" and "Northampton Sands". The shallow warm seas provided the material for the Bath and Cotswold Limestones. What is now Southern Germany was covered with warm, shallow sea. Some sort of chalky dust collected in the lagoons formed by coral reefs there. Mixed with water, this dust formed a white pasty substance which dried out at intervals. This paste proved to be an ideal material for preserving animals that fell into it. It is thanks to this area of what later became lithographic limestone, at Solnhofen, that we have such clear evidence of many of the creatures that lived at that time. If you look at the photograph on page 68 you will see that even the impression of the feathers of a bird were perfectly preserved.

What else should we see if we looked back into those swampy plains? The abundant vegetation included forests of conifers like our fir trees, cycads looking rather like present-day palms, and strange maidenhair trees which now exist only in Japan and China. It is strange to think of all these plants and trees without flowers, but that was how it was. A few of the cycads bore cones that looked like flowers, but we must wait for the Cretaceous period before we see real ones.

In amongst the plants we would find all the Triassic insects, still busy. Dragonflies still thrived and so did grasshoppers and beetles. Now they had been joined by the ant family and several new types of fly. The great number of ponds and lakes had given rise to a huge population of freshwater snails. There were so many of them in some places that their shells formed special beds of limestone, like the Purbeck Marble of Dorset.

However, it was on the land and in the air that the real excitement lay. We shall find some of the biggest ever dinosaurs in this period, like the eighty-five foot *Diplodocus* and *Brontosaurus*. The fierce flesh-eating *Allosaurs* and *Megalosaurs* were terrifying their smaller relatives as well as the plant eaters. Strange-looking armoured dinosaurs like *Stegosaurus* plodded about, browsing off plants.

For the first time there were creatures in the air, other than insects. The *Pterosaurs* had grown a skin web between their fingers, and had learned to fly. They must have looked incredible soaring through the sky. They were not alone, however. That fossil bird *Archaeopteryx* had joined them, having changed his scales for feathers over a long period of time.

Both the *Pterosaurs* and *Archaeopteryx*, however, fell prey to some of the sea reptiles. The incredible *Plesiosaurs* with their long, snaky necks could snatch these creatures out of the sky. In the water the *Ichthyosaurs*, so well adapted to their marine life, took their toll of the smaller fish and sea creatures. Some of these sea creatures would be acceptable as food even to us, for in this period we find the first oysters and crabs and even a sort of lobster. Ammonites of various sorts were common all over the world (they are now used to compare the rocks of one country with those of another).

The promise of the mammal-like reptiles of the Triassic period had not been fulfilled. They had come and gone. There were no large mammals in this Jurassic landscape but lurking in the undergrowth were no less than four types of true mammal. Small and inconspicuous at this stage, they were to grow and develop over the next 100 million years in such a way that when the dinosaurs disappeared, they took over. However, at this stage in our story the real dinosaurs have not even come, let alone disappeared, so let us return to them.

Freshwater snails. Below: lobster, crab and oyster.

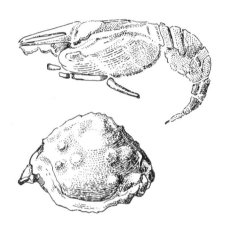

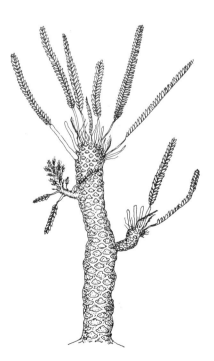

Diplodocus, *an 85 foot long swamp-dwelling dinosaur who lived 150 million years ago in the Jurassic period. Weighing over ten tons, it left the water only to lay eggs. Its remains are found in N. America, but it had a close relative,* **Cetiosaurus** *who lived in England.*

Above: **Diplodocus's** *neck vertebrae with cavities. Below: his reptile hip.*

Part of **Diplodocus's** *tail, designed for flexibility.*

The giants in the swamp

In this Jurassic period there was such a variety of dinosaurs that we need to divide them up. It is much easier to study all the dinosaurs of one type together because they had a great deal in common that only needs to be said once. We can then give more thought to the particular differences between basically similar animals.

Of all the animals that we shall study in this book, none were so fantastic as the group known as *Sauropods* (reptile feet). This group includes not only the biggest of all the dinosaurs, but, with the exception of the Blue Whale, the biggest animals that have ever lived on earth.

These *Sauropods* were probably descended from the *Plateosaurs* of the previous period. The twenty foot *Plateosaur*, weighing about the same as a full-grown rhinoceros, already went down on all fours to browse or catch his prey. It seems likely that as the *Sauropods* grew heavier, they spent more and more time on all fours. Eventually, it became impossible for them to stand on two feet at all.

However, with one exception they retained the feature of having their front legs shorter than their back legs.

All this group of *Sauropods* shared certain common features. They all had a massive body, supported on sturdy legs like tree trunks. Their necks were long and their heads small. They had long, or very long, tails, some of them with a whiplash end. Their feet were squat and heavy, with three claws on the back ones and one claw on the front ones. Their jaws were equipped with peg-shaped or flat teeth. These were very suitable for eating the plants and roots that provided most of their food. All these features they had in common, but what of the individuals?

Perhaps the best known is *Brontosaurus* (thunder reptile) whose correct name is *Apatosaurus*. Whenever you mention dinosaurs, people immediately think of *Brontosaurus*. Like most of his relatives, he lived in the shallow-water swamps that were so

Above: skeleton of **Diplodocus** *showing clearly the long whiplash tail, the open tracery of the neck vertebrae and the strong leg and shoulder bones. Below: skull of* **Diplodocus** *showing the typical plant-eaters teeth and the high narrow forehead.*

common in Jurassic times. Nose to tail, he was nearly seventy feet long and probably turned the scales at about thirty tons. To help you imagine that weight, a fully-grown elephant weighs about five tons. *Brontosaurus* spent most of his time in the water, where some of his colossal weight was supported for him. He was obliged to come ashore to lay eggs, and there his slow movement and ponderous walk made him an easy prey for some of the carnivorous dinosaurs of the time. You can see an illustration of this on page 51.

Brontosaurus may have been huge, but *Diplodocus* illustrated on page 46 was even longer, although he was much lighter in weight. Some of the skeletons of *Diplodocus* are over eighty feet long. Individual leg bones that have been found suggest that some specimens were even longer than this: possibly as much as one hundred feet. Of this enormous length, a large part is accounted for by the very long tail with a whiplash end. Apart from his sheer size, this tail was the only form of defence *Diplodocus* had. Being so much slimmer than his relative, *Brontosaurus*, he probably weighed a mere ten tons or so.

One of the exceptions to the "short front legs" rule was *Brachiosaurus* (arm reptile). He was seventy-five feet long, but with his long front legs he stood twenty feet high at the shoulder. When you add his very long neck to this, the top of his head was forty feet above the ground! Think of it; if you could stand three double-decker buses one on top of the other, *Brachiosaurus* would have his feet on the floor of the bottom one and his head bumping the uppermost ceiling of the top one. With his nostrils high on his head, he undoubtedly used his great height to stand in deep water where he was safe from his enemies.

In Europe there lived *Camarasaurus*, a sixty foot *Sauropod* who shows very clearly the typical combination of heavy limbs and very open, almost delicate, vertebrae. This brings us to a series of very interesting features of the *Sauropods*.

As their weight increased, the slender hollow

ALLOSAURUS

BRONTOSAURUS

NOSTRIL

bones of their ancestors became inadequate. Their leg bones got thicker and heavier to carry their increased weight. The legs themselves became straighter, so that they acted like pillars supporting the heavy body. With large spongy pads underneath the foot bones, these feet could take the weight of several tons that came down on them as the animal walked.

In order to avoid the weight of heavy bone where it wasn't necessary, the vertebrae and the skull developed holes and cavities. The internal structure became a lattice of delicate supporting ribs, thickening only where they had to take strain or pressure. It is instructive to compare these vertebrae with some examples of modern reinforced concrete architecture. There is a striking similarity.

It is very noticeable that the *Sauropods* had small skulls. If you try lifting a weight of several pounds with your arm at full stretch you will quickly discover one of the reasons. It would have been impossible to carry a large head at the end of a twenty or thirty foot slender neck. As it was, the *Sauropods* had a very tough, cable-like ligament running along the top of their neck vertebrae, just to move that slender neck and small head.

This small head created problems. You can only have a fairly small mouth and jaw in such a head. This restricts the size of object you can bite, and the amount you can take in at one bite. *Sauropods'* teeth could only have coped with vegetable matter, and fairly soft material at that. Plant food is not as nutritious as meat, so an animal has to eat a lot more of it to get the same benefit. Our present-day cows and elephants spend a large part of the day eating in order to get enough nourishment from their vegetable diet. The *Sauropods* must have had to do much the same to keep their enormous bodies supplied. They had the advantage of many reptiles, in that being cold-blooded and comparatively slow-moving, they didn't need the supply of food that an active mammal needs. Even so, it is still something of a puzzle how these enormous animals found

BRACHIOSAURUS

Above: how water supported sauropods' great weight. Below: marble formed from fossilised snail shells. Bottom: Jurassic insects.

enough food of sufficiently nutritious quality.

One or two other points about these *Sauropods* are worth noting. In their small heads they only had room for equally small brains. That seventy or eighty foot of giant was controlled by a brain about the size of your fist! Fortunately, in the region of the hips there was a big nerve centre which helped to control all the back half of the animal. It is possible that some reactions were controlled automatically from this centre. This would avoid every message from the senses having to make the long journey up the spinal nerve to the brain, and would produce faster reactions to attack.

Here we leave the giants of the swampland, browsing happily off plants and roots. Their size and their life in the water protected them most of the time from the fierce predators at which we are now going to look.

Flesh-eating monsters

While the *Sauropods* inhabited the swamps and shallow lakes, the drier land was dominated by a group of dinosaurs known as *Theropoda* (bird feet). Although they all belonged to the same group, they varied tremendously in size and the way they lived. In fact their bird-like feet and their habit of walking on two legs were about the only things they had in common. The most remarkable of the *Theropoda* are certainly the *Carnosaurs* (meat reptiles). It is a little difficult to believe when you compare them, but these frightening beasts almost certainly evolved from the little *Procompsognathus* of the Triassic period.

Over the years, the *Carnosaurs* had grown in size and strength. They had lost the hollow, lightweight bones of their ancestors, which were too weak to carry the increased weight. Their skulls had grown much larger. To reduce the weight of bone, they had developed the open lattice structure that we saw in the *Sauropods*. Their jaws are terrifying. They have a formidable set of backward-curving, blade-like teeth, and the hinge is so formed that the jaw can gape. That is, the jaws can open to an incredible width so that large pieces of meat can be swallowed whole. In fact, the whole of the *Carnosaur's* head was capable of expanding a little at the joints.

As though these jaws were not enough, the *Carno-saurs* had long claws on their three-fingered hands. The arms themselves were short but powerful. We

Below: **Cetiosaurus**, *a 60 foot long swamp-dwelling dinosaur. He lived in the Midlands and Southern England 150 million years ago. He was very similar to the N. American* **Diplodocus** *in build and way of life.*

Below: the foot and hand of a Jurassic allosaur, with long claws on both.

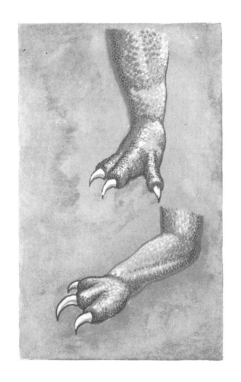

can picture one of these *Carnosaurs*, like *Allosaurus*, attacking *Brontosaurus* with slashing claws ripping and tearing, while long and terrible jaws sank razor teeth into his flesh. When this armoury was backed by two or three tons of powerful body, you can see what a formidable predator a *Carnosaur* was.

Allosaurus was typical of the whole group of *Carnosaurs*. He was about thirty feet long, with a powerful, massive body. More than half of his length was in his tail, which he used as a counter-balance. Like all the dinosaurs who had large heads, he had a short, strong neck. His size of head couldn't possibly have been supported at the end of a long neck such as *Diplodocus* had. In order to stand on two feet, *Allosaurus* had also had to develop a stronger pelvis. The hip bone had to have a deeper socket, and the attachment of the pelvis to the vertebrae had to be stronger. You can see both these points illustrated in the photograph above.

The Jurassic *Carnosaurs* from different parts of

*The skeleton of **Antrodemus**, a typical Jurassic allosaur. This great carnivorous dinosaur, over thirty feet long, lived in N. America 140 million years ago. You can see the jaw hinge, the open structure of the head and the wicked curved teeth. Over half his length was* *taken up by his tail, which was needed to balance his massive body. His teeth, coupled with his clawed hands and feet made him one of the most effective meat-eating dinosaurs that ever lived. Compare him with **Tyrannosaurus**,* *on page 74 in Chapter 5.*

Below: **Ceratosaurus,** *the meat-eater with a horn on the end of his nose.*

Top: **Compsognathus,** *the turkey-sized carnivore. Above:* **Ornitholestes,** *the 6 foot carnivore from N. America. These two are typical of the lighter Jurassic carnivores. Below: the "fingers" of* **Ornitholestes.**

the world were so similar that it would be tedious to describe them all. One who is notable is the twenty foot North American *Ceratosaurus,* for he had a horn on the end of his nose and a five-fingered hand. Normally the carnivorous animals had no defensive equipment of this sort. They were usually doing the attacking. They relied on their strength and speed to keep them out of trouble. We expect to find armour and horns on the plant eaters, whose browsing way of life left them constantly open to attack, but not on the predators.

Although we have looked at the most spectacular *Carnosaurs* first, they were by no means the only ones which inhabited the Jurassic lands. There were many smaller, lighter animals which remained much closer to their Triassic predecessors in size and appearance. They varied in size from a few feet to ten feet at their maximum.

Two examples are enough to illustrate what they were like. *Compsognathus* was a European dinosaur whose claim to fame lies largely in his small size! He was no bigger than a turkey, but was light and fast on his two feet, with a long flexible tail to help him keep his balance. He had three fingers on his hand, and four toes on his feet. His fourth toe, however, pointed backwards rather like some birds' feet. He probably lived on small lizards, some of the small mammals and various insects.

In North America a similar dinosaur was found called *Ornitholestes* (bird catcher). He was given his name because his build, and especially his hands, suggested that he might have lived on birds. This is possible but not likely. He probably lived on much the same diet as *Compsognathus. Ornitholestes* was about six feet long, with a small head set on a moderately long neck. He had a good set of sharp teeth, as we might expect in a carnivorous dinosaur. Side by side with big brother *Allosaurus* (but probably keeping well out of his way) we find many small dinosaurs like *Ornitholestes.*

Even these two groups of animals, the large and the small carnivores, didn't have the land to themselves. Towards the end of the Jurassic period we find some newcomers on the scene. These are the other type of dinosaur that we mentioned briefly earlier on. They are *Ornithischians* (bird hips). Their pelvis is made more like a bird's and less like a reptile's. Unlike the *Sauropods* and *Theropods*, there is no evolutionary line to trace how these animals developed from their thecodont ancestors. They just appeared. It is possible that the stages in between have not yet been found as fossils – or perhaps the fossil remains have been broken into so many fragments that no one has put the jigsaw puzzle together properly.

Since we shall be seeing quite a lot of the bird-hip group of dinosaurs in the next chapter, it is worth looking at them in general before we look at individuals. If you look back at the diagram on page 33 you can remind yourself of what is meant by bird-hip. As well as this feature, the group had a number of other things in common. They were all plant eaters, as we can tell from their teeth. Most of them had no front teeth, but often had instead some form of beak. Their arms, although not long, were well developed and obviously played an important role in eating and getting about. None of them grew to the size of either the *Sauropods* or the *Carnosaurs*.

Top: bipedal dinosaurs used the weight of their tail to balance their big head. Above: **Ceratosaurus's** *head with its unusual horn. Below:* **Allosaurus** *at work on the carcase of a plant-eater he has killed.*

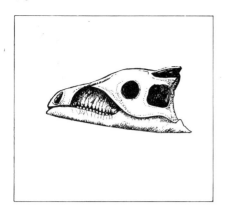

Above: **Hypsilophodon.** *Skull showing the light structure suited to plant eating. Below: skeleton complete.*

In the photograph above and the detail below, you can see **Hypsilophodon's** *feet, well suited to tree-living.*

One of the first members of this group to be found was *Hypsilophodon*. His long name is derived from the peculiar teeth that he had, which had strange folds in them. Just to be awkward, he is one of the exceptions which did have teeth in the front of his jaw. He was about five or six feet long with well-developed hands. Although he had five fingers, only four of them were any use to him. The fifth one was short and stubby and stuck out near his wrist. He had four toes, all pointing forwards, unlike the *Theropods* who often had the more bird-like three-toed foot, with the fourth toe at the back.

Hypsilophodon's arrangement of teeth and his hands and feet have led scientists to think that he probably lived in the trees, rather like a modern tree kangaroo. His hands would certainly have been well adapted to gripping leaves, and his toes would have provided him with a good grip on branches.

In contrast to the small-sized *Hypsilophodon* was *Camptosaurus*, who grew to fifteen feet. Skeletons of this dinosaur turn up both in Europe and North America. Some of the best examples were found in the "Morrison Beds" in North America. Here there were specimens ranging in size from four to fifteen feet. No one is certain whether these were different members of a group, or whether the small skeletons are the young animals and the big ones the adults. All the skeletons were very similar in structure, so they were at least very closely related.

Camptosaurus was a typical *Ornithopod* (bird foot). He had no teeth at the front of his mouth, but those further back, called cheek teeth, were well developed. This makes it clear that he was a plant eater like the rest of the *Ornithopods*. He had longer arms than many dinosaurs of this type, and it is likely that he used them partly for support when browsing. An interesting feature of *Camptosaurus* was his claws which were short and rather like baby hoofs. His tail was shorter in proportion to his body than that of many of his relatives. Without the counterbalance effect of a long tail, he must have stood more upright than the small dinosaurs of this group. This more upright posture will be even more noticeable in the *Iguanodons* of the next period, who were closely related to *Camptosaurus*.

The armoured brigade

We have seen earlier how vulnerable the plant eating dinosaurs were. Few of them in previous periods had much in the way of protection or defence. The *Sauropods* relied on their size and their life in the water; others had to rely on speed, and possibly some form of camouflage. It is possible that *Hypsilophodon* took to the lower branches of trees to gain

In this reconstruction you can see **Hypsilophodon** *in typical surroundings. Note how he uses his feet to hold on to the branch, leaving his hands free.*

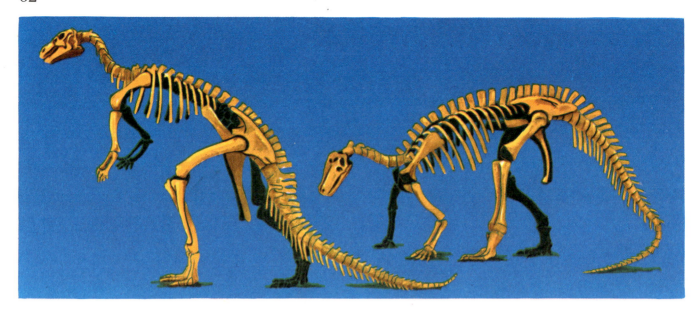

some cover and protection from his enemies.

Here in the Jurassic period we find the first of a series of armoured dinosaurs. *Scelidosaurus*, from the Lower Jurassic period, was about twelve feet long and had bony plates down his back. These extended all the way from his head to the tip of his tail. He belonged to the bird-hip group, but walked on all fours. He had the typical high hip and low shoulder appearance of the bipeds who had become quadrupeds. He was typical of all the *Stegosaurs*, (plated reptiles) in having a heavy body set on short strong legs. His head was noticeably small, with the weak jaw and grinding teeth that we have come to expect in the plant eaters.

These bony plates sticking up from *Scelidosaurus'* back must have made him look like a very coarse saw in silhouette. Whether they provided any real protection is somewhat doubtful. Certainly they must have been rather daunting to the carnivores who preyed on him. If you can frighten your enemies away by your appearance, at least it gives you some protection.

From this beginning there evolved a dinosaur with a rather more formidable set of armour plates. If you look at page 65 you will see what a remarkable animal *Stegosaurus* was. Twenty feet long and eight or ten feet high at the hip, *Stegosaurus* was an astonishing sight in this Jurassic scene. The two pairs of long spikes on the end of his tail undoubtedly

Above: **Camptosaurus** *in a typical walking and browsing posture. You can see how he used his strong front legs for support.* **Camptosaurus's** *skull below, with its beak-like front.*

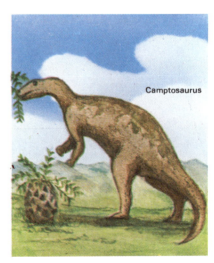

Camptosaurus

Above: reconstruction of **Camptosaurus** *as he probably appeared in life, standing rather upright.*

STEGOSAURUS

Above: reconstruction of **Scelidosaurus**, *the 12 foot early armoured dinosaur. You can see the set of protective plates that he wore down his back.*

In the illustration below you can see how the bony plates were set in a line above **Scelidosaurus's** *pelvis. Notice the length of this bone and the thick leg bone.*

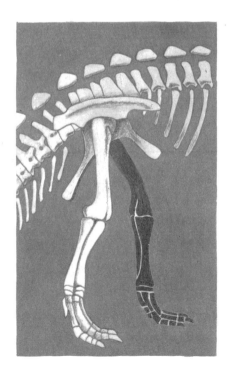

provided him with a deadly weapon. Perhaps this was as well, for the bony plates sticking up along his back were only of limited use. They protected the vital spinal cord, but left his sides wide open to attack, unless he could fend off his attacker by lashing his tail about.

Having the hind legs much longer than the front ones gave *Stegosaurus* a rather odd shape. His body sloped downwards from the hip in a long curve to the small head, which was carried quite close to the ground on a short neck. The tail took up only about seven or eight feet of his total length, but had powerful muscles that could swing it both upwards and from side to side. His hind feet had three short stubby nails, and were thick and squat. They also had a thick pad of spongy tissue underneath, to cushion the bones against the two tons of weight that came down on them when the animal walked. Like the *Sauropods*, *Stegosaurus* had developed a rather straight back leg to support his massive body, but his elbows still stuck out a bit, as they did in the earlier reptiles. These front legs were much slimmer than the back ones, having less weight to support, and had five stubby claws like little hoofs.

Like many of the swamp dwellers, *Stegosaurus* had only a tiny brain but a big nerve centre in his hips. There is a funny poem that tries to suggest that he had two brains, but of course this wasn't true. Like the *Sauropods* he just had a lot of nerves coming

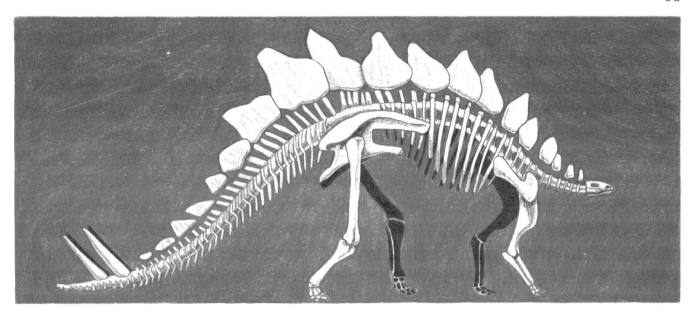

together at one place, because his hind quarters were so massive they took a lot of controlling. This nerve centre was rather like a lot of railway lines joining up outside a mainline station. It looks very complicated and important, but it is all controlled by quite a small signal box. *Stegosaurus's* brain was the signal box, and the nerve centre in his hip was only the junction. He would be a strange and to us, rather comic sight, plodding slowly about that Jurassic landscape. Nibbling small plants with his little beak-like mouth, he would keep a careful eye on those fierce meat eating relatives of his. They must have fancied that large body as providing some succulent lunch, but perhaps they were a little apprehensive of those big bony plates and that fearsome spiked tail.

In time, however, this impressive looking armour (or the ability of *Stegosaurus* to adapt to changing conditions) proved inadequate. He only survived into the early part of the next period, and then became extinct. He roamed the earth for forty or fifty million years, however, which is not a bad innings even for a dinosaur.

Stand by for takeoff

If *Stegosaurus* had chosen to look up into the air, he would have seen the first flying reptiles! In this period we shall see the first fossils of both flying reptiles and true birds, and very strange some of

Above: **Stegosaurus** *skeleton with its impressive rows of armour plates. Below: the elephant-like feet of* **Stegosaurus** *with their short stubby nails.*

In this reconstruction you can see how the plates on **Stegosaurus's** *back were set at an angle and alternated.*

them looked too. But before we look at the creatures themselves, we need to consider how any creature can fly.

For any object to overcome the pull of the earth and rise into the air, there must be a certain relationship between the weight of the object and the power which is lifting it. This applies whether we are talking of a small bird, or the latest lunar rocket. If the object is heavy, like an aeroplane or a large bird, then you must have either a powerful engine or powerful shoulder muscles to lift it. Small birds and bats with very light bodies can manage with comparatively slight shoulder muscles. Butterflies, with a tiny body and a large wingspan, are even better provided for.

This question of wingspan in birds and animals is important. Ignoring the power-driven fliers, flying animals that provide their own power have a number of common factors. Their wing area is large compared with their body size. Their shoulder and chest muscles and bones are specially adapted for flying, and usually their bones are light and hollow to reduce weight. If you look at a number of different birds and animals you will discover that the best fliers are those with a large spread of wings compared with their body size and weight. Heavy birds with small wings, like chickens or ostriches, fly poorly or not at all.

We have seen that, in many of the prehistoric

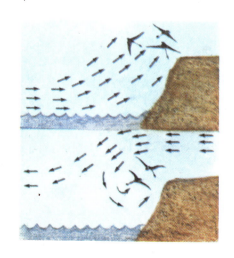

Top: **Stegosaurus** *nerve supply reconstruction. Above: pterosaur wing structure. Below: rising air currents used by pterosaurs.*

RHAMPHORINCHUS

Above: reconstruction of long tailed pterosaur. Below: Bat wing structure for comparison.

animals, there is a desperate shortage of evidence about their early development. This is again true of the flying reptiles or *Pterosaurs*. We can only make intelligent guesses. It is likely that some of the early tree-living dinosaurs grew skin webs to help them leap from branch to branch. These primitive webs would have perished when the animal died and only its bones would have become fossilised. Hence the lack of evidence.

We therefore have to accept the fossils of flying reptiles that were already fully developed and capable of flight. What did they look like and how did they fly? The first and most important point to notice is that the skin web that served as a wing is supported at the front edge by the arm, and then by a very overgrown fourth finger. This finger was in fact much longer than the arm itself. At the back, the wing was attached to the ankle, leaving the foot free. The remaining three fingers of the four-fingered hand stuck out in front of the wing in a most odd way, as you can see from the illustration on page 66.

Each of these "spare" fingers had a claw, and was probably used for holding on to rocks or trees. The five-toed foot also had claws, which were used for perching. Certainly the construction of the animal meant that it could not walk on its two feet, although it may perhaps have been able to pull itself along in some awkward fashion.

The similarity of the *Pterosaur* wing to a glider

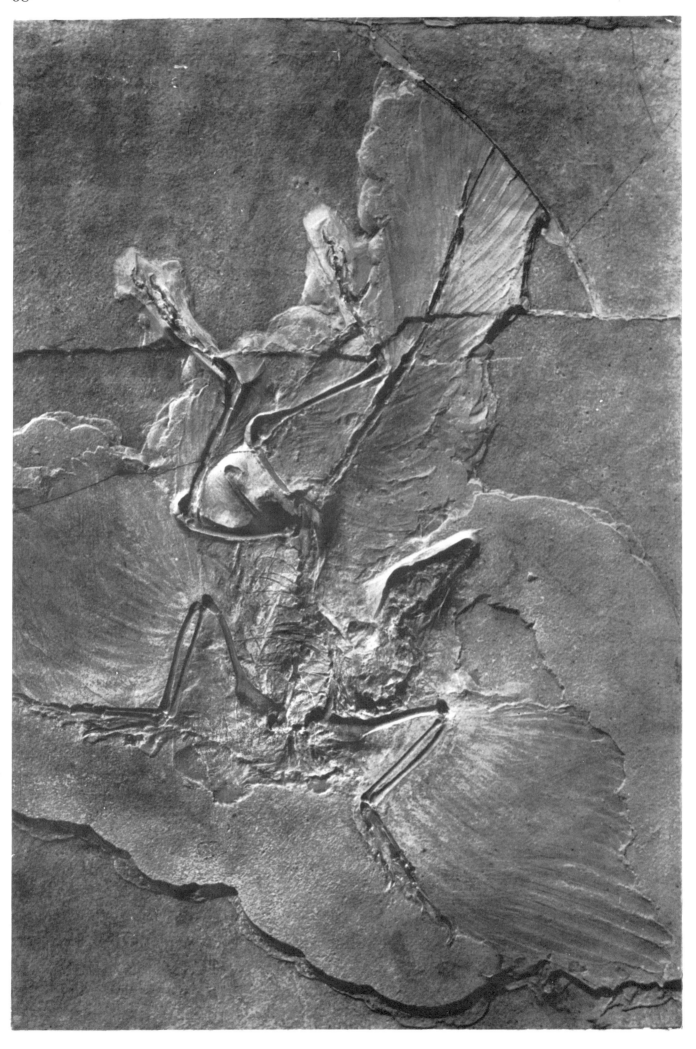

Above: the skull of **Archae-opteryx***, showing its similarity to a reptile skull.*

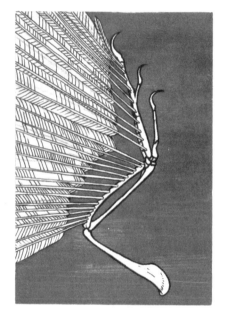

Archaeopteryx *wing, showing residual claws and feathers.*

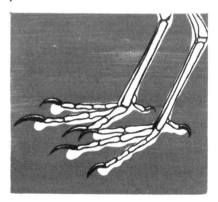

Reconstruction of **Archae-opteryx** *feet. Notice the similarity to the feet of some bipedal dinosaurs. Page 68. The original fossil of* **Archaeopteryx** *embedded in lithographic stone.*

wing is significant. A glider depends on upward currents of air for its ability to fly. The *Pterosaurs* had rather poorly-developed flying muscles, and must also have depended a great deal on gliding on rising currents of air.

Rhamphorhynchus (prow-beak) was typical of the early *Pterosaurs*. He had a three-foot wing span and a small body but rather a large head. He had a good set of sharp teeth, which pointed forwards and would have been very effective for catching fish. At the end of his long tail he had a diamond-shaped rudder which helped him to steer and manoeuvre. As a change from the land dinosaurs, he had quite a large brain for his size.

Flying involves going up and down as well as forwards and sideways. It also means keeping your balance in the air. The co-ordination of all these complicated actions obviously needed a better, bigger brain. We shall see this demonstrated even more markedly in the birds later in the chapter.

Later in the Jurassic period a new flying reptile appeared, called a *Pterodactyl*. When we come across these in story books, they are often made out to be huge creatures, but the early ones were only seven or eight inches long. They had a short tail instead of the long one that the earlier *Pterosaurs* had, and their teeth were smaller and fewer and were set in a more pointed sort of beak. Here we can see the move towards the toothless beak of the later birds, including our present ones.

The effort of flying, as we have seen, requires a well-developed brain. It also requires other things like a good supply of oxygen. This means a more efficient heart and lungs. Once up in the air, it becomes necessary to control the body temperature to offset variations in the warmth of the atmosphere. This involves some sort of covering to insulate the animal and prevent it losing heat, or getting too hot. The *Pterosaurs* had made a start on all these adaptations, as far as we are able to judge. It was left to *Archaeopteryx*, the first bird to complete the process.

Thanks to those lagoons at Solnhofen that we

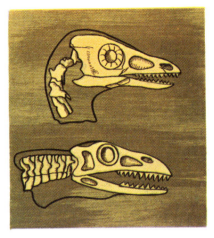

Comparison of the skull of **Archaeopteryx** *with that of* **Saltoposuchus**.

Pterosaurs use the higher wind speeds at 100 feet to gain power for their dive.

Reconstruction of Jurassic short-tailed **Pterodactyl***, with a more pointed beak.*

mentioned earlier, we have a beautiful fossil record of *Archaeopteryx*, full of detail. You can see a photograph of it on page 68. Somewhere along the evolutionary line, the flying reptiles had branched off and developed feathers. This solved their problem of controlling body temperature, for feathers are very good insulators. We must assume that *Archaeopteryx* had also become warm blooded and no longer really belonged to the cold blooded reptiles.

He still had a lot of reptile features, though. He carried his three spare claws on the leading edge of his wing just like the *Pterosaurs*. He had a long, rather reptile-like tail with the feathers set flat on either side unlike those of modern birds. He still had teeth in his jaws, which modern birds don't have, and the finger bones inside his wing were clearly separate. In modern birds they are fused together.

He was undoubtedly a bird, though, and not a reptile. He was about the size of our present-day pigeon, and walked about and stood on two well-developed legs. He probably lived in woodlands, or at least in trees, unlike the *Pterosaurs*. His diet probably consisted of grubs and insects and some of the small woodland creatures. Between the insects, the birds and the *Pterosaurs* and *Pterodactyls*, the Jurassic skies were becoming quite busy.

This move of the reptiles into the air was a dramatic breakthrough. It was comparable in many ways to the move of the lobe-finned fish on to the land. A new dimension had been conquered, a new environment created. We cannot now imagine the sky without birds in it. In prehistory terms, it must have been the equivalent of the first man landing on the moon in our day and age.

Our ancestors: the first mammals

The appearance and later disappearance of the mammal-like reptiles in an earlier age was very disappointing. In this period, however, we have definite evidence of early true mammals. As we have repeatedly discovered, the evidence is truly fragmentary. It is only thanks to the genius and the persistence of scientists who have pieced together the small clues that are available, that we know so much about these early mammals.

Let us first remind ourselves what true mammals are. They are warm blooded creatures. That is, they live at a higher temperature and a faster pace than the cold blooded reptiles. This means they need more food to keep them going. They need some way of maintaining an even body temperature, and so have to use fur or feathers to insulate themselves against changing temperatures. Because they use more oxygen to maintain their faster rate of living (called metabolic rate) mammals also need a more complex heart. For preference, they need one with four chambers to keep the oxygen-rich blood separate from the de-oxygenated blood. Finally, mammals normally suckle their babies.

Reconstruction of **Archaeopteryx** *in flight. Notice the rather scaly neck, the claws on the front edge of the wing, and the long claws on the feet.*

ARCHAEOPTERYX

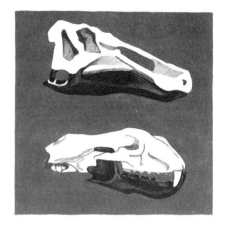

Above: reptile skull at top has jaw in three pieces; mammal jaw is in one piece.

Above: duckbilled platypus, modern descendant of the Jurassic small mammals.

Modern scaly ant eater.

Now, most of these differences are lost when an animal is fossilized. Apart from the fur or feathers that are sometimes recorded, scientists have to rely on other evidence. This they find in the construction of the jaw bones. Reptiles have a jaw which is connected to the skull by several little bones. Mammals have just one lower jaw bone, and the little bones left over have moved into the ear. Here they form part of the system that transmits sound to the ear drum. Happily this evidence is usually preserved and so we can say with some confidence that this animal was a mammal, and that one was not.

These methods were used to decide that several small animals in the Jurassic period were mammals. The first was a small animal called a *Decodont*. He was an insect eater and was probably the ancestor of our present-day scaly ant eater and duck billed platypus. The second was a *Triconodont* who was about the size of a small fox. He was a carnivore, judging from his teeth and lived on the small animals and reptiles that inhabited the undergrowth. The third group were called *Pantotheres*. They existed in the form of insect eaters and meat eaters. They were probably small furry animals and could be anything from the size of a rat to the size of a small terrier. They were important, being the ancestors of all present-day mammals, including ourselves.

The remains of these creatures are such that the intelligent guesses here outweigh the information. We can only adopt the now familiar technique of using our knowledge of present-day animals to reclothe those ancient fossil bones with flesh. Modern techniques of studying fossil remains may in time give us more information on these early animals, and confirm or destroy our guesses.

Down to the sea again

Although this period produced such an exciting range of animals on land and in the air, it should not be imagined that the sea was uninteresting. We have already looked at the superb adaptation of the *Ichthyosaurs* to their sea life. In this Jurassic period these fish lizards rose to the peak of their development. They ranged in size from six to thirty feet long and hunted in the Jurassic seas in large numbers. Their fossil remains, with slight variations, are found all over the world. They must have been a constant source of terror to the shoals of smaller fish, which by this time looked very like our present sea population. One of the creatures who was noticeable by his absence was the whale, which was a much later development in the sea mammals.

The *Ichthyosaurs* were kept company by a group of sea crocodiles called *Teleosaurs,* who grew to the astonishing length of fifty feet. They had the strange habit of swallowing stones to help them digest their food. These stones, known as "gastroliths" give us a good guide to their diet, for they are found stained with the "ink" that squids squirt out. It is fairly safe to assume that squids comprised a large proportion of their diet.

The *Teleosaurs* may have been the ancestors of the *Geosaurs* who appeared later in the Jurassic period. These crocodiles had also adapted themselves to sea life. Their legs and arms look rather like those of seals and their tail has changed to make swimming easier. They must have competed with the *Ichthyosaurs* for their diet of fish and other small marine life. Their adaptation doesn't seem to have been wholly successful, however, for they became extinct early in the Cretaceous period that is to follow.

As this Jurassic period draws to a close, we find the seas retreating once more, leaving "land bridges" between continents and exposing sea beds. The world is populated by a vast range of animals, flying reptiles, birds and sea creatures. Some of them are already at their peak and will disappear rapidly at the beginning of the next period. Others, like the mammals, are just flexing their muscles for the struggle to come. As geological period follows period there is a constantly changing pattern of living things to be found. Changes in climate and geography encourage some and discourage others. There is never a time when everything stands still.

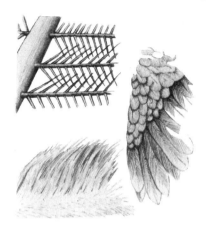

Above: barbs of individual feather, layers of feathers and fur act as insulators.

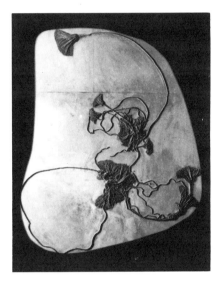

Above: fossil of sea lily a beautiful marine creature from the Jurassic seas.

Above: **Ophthalmosaurus,** *a Jurassic ichthyosaur with a greatly enlarged eye and broad flexible paddles.*

TYRANNOSAURUS

Exit the giants

Above: magnolia, one of the early Cretaceous flowers.

sea areas } in Upper Cretaceous
land areas

Above: the changing pattern of Cretaceous sea and land.

Above: the first snakes to appear turn up in this period, like the boa constrictor shown here.

135 million years ago in the Cretaceous period

THE position and extent of the seas and oceans affected every living thing. They controlled how much land was available for creatures to live on. They brought rain and water to vast desert areas, and exposed great sea beds to become deserts and land areas in their turn. They divided enormous continents, sometimes reducing them to a series of small islands. We find that at times Britain was joined to France, at times to Scandinavia and sometimes completely submerged under the sea. At one time Africa and South America were joined and most of the land area of Russia was under water.

The development of prehistoric animals was closely linked with climate and food supplies. It is impossible to make sense of the changes that took place without some knowledge of the background. Let's see therefore what the sea was doing in this period. The withdrawal of the sea at the end of the Jurassic period had left a great big piece of land that included England and France and Northern and Central Europe. On the Southern edge of this a trench began to form, into which the many slow moving rivers washed silt and mud – and dinosaurs!

Along a strip from southern England across Belgium there are areas rich in Early Cretaceous fossils. In geological terms this large land area was destined to last only a short time. The sea began to rise again and eventually, in the later part of the Lower Cretaceous, broke through to cut Britain off from the Continent. The climate of Europe changed; there and also over much of North America, the weather became milder with more marked differences between the seasons.

Although the land areas had been drastically reduced, they were teeming with life. Birds and *Pterosaurs* flew to and fro in search of food in the new

Above: the Wealden strip that ran from S. England across the continent.

Above: sea urchins and squids in the sea.

Above: **Archelon,** *a twelve foot turtle who swam in the Cretaceous seas in many parts of the world.*

deciduous trees, like oak and poplar and plane. *Hypsilophodon* perched here and the first big snakes, like boa constrictors, lay coiled in wait for their prey. Flowering plants appeared, together with a host of insects to pollinate them.

Sea urchins, squids and shellfish provided almost unlimited food for the sea reptiles like crocodiles, *Mosasaurs* and the newly-developed *Elasmosaurus.* Turtles had returned to the sea and grown large, while *Ichthyosaurs*, in spite of their superb adaptation, were extinct well before the end of the period.

On the land, our large *Sauropod* friends like *Brontosaurus* and *Diplodocus* were still sheltering quietly in swamplands and shallow water. They were joined by a group of animals called *Hadrosaurs,* who all looked as if they were wearing party hats! On the drier land, the carnivorous dinosaurs grew and developed. What we shall do is look at the newcomers like *Tyrannosaurus* and *Gorgosaurus* amongst the big carnivores, and at the weird developments amongst the armoured dinosaurs like *Ankylosaurus.* The almost delicate running form of *Orinithomimus*, the ostrich dinosaur, will contrast with the great weight of the horned dinosaurs.

In the air we shall see the earlier *Pterosaurs* supplanted by the impressive *Pteranodon.* We shall see how the swimming and diving birds came to keep *Archaeopteryx* company. We shall glance at the teeming life of the sea, and in the undergrowth will plot the progress of the true mammals. Having introduced them all we shall then – incredibly – say goodbye to them, for by the end of the period they were all extinct except for the mammals.

With their feet on the ground

Amongst the exciting finds that came out of that Wealden strip that stretched from southern England across the continent were a whole herd of dinosaurs called *Iguanodons* (iguana teeth). These were similar in many ways to *Camptosaurus* in Chapter four. They were about twenty-five to thirty feet long, and stood about twelve to fourteen feet tall.

Iguanodon had stronger front legs than *Camptosaurus*. Not only were his arms stronger, but he had a very unusual feature; his equivalent of our thumb had become a sharp spike. As a plant eater, he needed some protection and this spike presumably provided it. When his skeleton was first discovered the scientists assumed that this spike. was a horn, and reconstructed him with it stuck on the end of his nose like *Ceratosaurus!*

The *Iguanodons* seem to have lived in herds, which was unusual amongst dinosaurs. Another interesting point about the herds was that there were no youngsters amongst them. Once hatched, the young apparently had to fend for themselves.

The second feature that is of particular interest is *Iguanodon's* teeth. Instead of having just one set, like many of the dinosaurs, he had rows of them set one above the other. This meant that when one tooth wore out, it fell out and was replaced by the next.

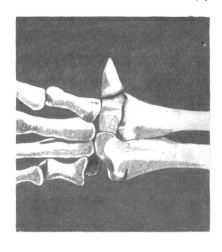

Above: **Iguanodon** *thumb.*
Below: Reconstruction and skeleton of **Iguanodon**.

The armoured dinosaurs

In looking at these creatures, we can't help thinking of knights in armour or early tanks. These dinosaurs had the same heavy, clumsy quality about them and even some similar weapons! The flailing tail of *Stegosaurus*, with its collection of terrifying spikes, and the great club on the end of *Ankylosaurus'* tail are surprisingly like the weapons the knights used when jousting. Even the animal armour had similarities. Some of these animals had big, saucer-shaped bony plates to protect them, while others had a multitude of small pieces of bone in a mosaic which acted like chain mail.

The first of these animals to catch our attention is *Polacanthus*. Like *Stegosaurus*, he was a heavy fourteen-foot beast with the characteristic high hip and low shoulder form. His most startling feature was the double row of spikes he carried from his neck to his hips. These varied from six to fifteen inches long and were set at an angle for better effect. From the hip joint to the tip of his tail, *Polacanthus*, like *Stegosaurus,* had pairs of plates.

Above: reconstruction of **Palaeoscincus**. *His spiked armour allowed him to live quietly in the undergrowth.*

Above: **Polacanthus** *as he appeared when alive. His 14 feet of armour gave effective protection.*

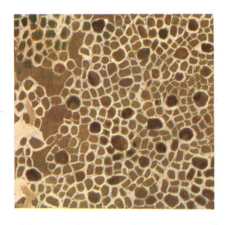

Above: the mosaic pattern of small bones on the back of **Nodosaurus**, *an armoured dinosaur. These animals had tiny teeth like beads and lived on very soft food.*

As was typical of the armoured brigade, he was a passive plant eater, with his weak teeth set in a small jaw. He had a very capacious body to hold the huge bulk of greenstuff that was needed to maintain such a heavy beast, and stout legs to transport him. He roamed the uplands of southern England and thrived happily for many millions of years.

The armoured dinosaurs appeared all over the world in varying forms and there is only space here to refer to a few of the more extraordinary ones. *Ankylosaurus* was typical of one sort in that he had big bony plates all over his back. His head was well protected by a thick bony roof to his skull, and his feet were broad and had short stubby nails. His great advantage, apart from his armour, was that he had a big heavy lump of bone, like a club, on the end of his tail. It must have been a very effective weapon when swung to and fro.

Palaeoscincus was similarly built except that, in addition to his armour, he had a set of wicked looking spikes sticking out on each side of his body. In combination with his club tail this made it very difficult for his predators to reach his only weak spot, which was his soft underbelly. He was almost impossible to overturn. His weight of several tons and his habit of crouching close to the ground helped a lot in this respect. The largest skeletons suggest that he grew to a length of twenty-five feet, but was only six feet high at the top of his shoulder.

In spite of their small heads, weak jaws and poor teeth, and the very large and heavy bodies they had to feed, the armoured dinosaurs thrived in the Cretaceous landscape. The precise type of armour they had varied from animal to animal. Whatever its form it was obviously effective, for they lived right through the long Cretaceous period of eighty million years.

The horned dinosaurs

There are so many exciting and incredible facts about the horned dinosaurs that it is very difficult not to plunge straight into a description of an

ANKYLOSAURUS

Above: **Ankylosaurus** *in Cretaceous times, protected by armour plates, spikes, and club-like tail illustrated below.*

individual animal. However we must curb our impatience and ask the question, "Where did they come from?"

The most likely answer is this: early in the Cretaceous period there was a strange looking dinosaur by the name of *Psittacosaurus*. It meant parrot reptile, and referred to the odd sort of beak this animal had. This three-foot animal was a fairly typical two-legged "bird-hip", except for his rather high narrow skull and his parrot beak. These two features are typical of all the horned dinosaurs who were known as *Ceratopsians* (with horns) and it seems likely that some relative of *Psittacosaurus*

Above: **Protoceratops**, *the first horned dinosaur.*

Above: **Monoclonius**, *with just one horn on his nose.*

Above: **Psittacosaurus**, *the probable ancestor of all the horned dinosaurs.*

was the ancestor of them all.

The first true *Ceratopsian, Protoceratops,* is fascinating for a particular reason. He was one of the first dinosaurs of whom we have examples all the way from newly-hatched to full grown adult. For the first time, it was possible to see how a particular dinosaur grew and developed. You can follow some of the details of this development on page 81.

Let us first see what the *Ceratopsians* had in common. They walked on all fours in spite of their two-legged ancestors. Like the armoured dinosaurs, they probably grew too heavy to remain upright. This was especially true when their heads grew bigger and bigger in proportion to their bodies. They all had four-toed feet and five-fingered "hands", although two of their fingers were rather short. Their back legs were noticeably longer than their front ones, like so many of the dinosaurs we have looked at.

Probably the most significant fact about *Ceratopsians* was the frill that grew back from their skulls over their neck and shoulders. This served two purposes. It provided an anchorage for the powerful muscles and tendons that were needed to support the heavy head. It also gave protection for the back of the neck, a very vital part of any animal's anatomy.

The number and arrangement of their horns varied, and we shall describe them as we look at the individual animals. They obviously used their horns to attack enemies such as *Gorgosaurus* and *Tyrannosaurus*. One look at that frightening collection of horns is enough to suggest what sort of damage this did to the carnivores. If you add to this the fact that the *Ceratopsians* almost certainly lived in herds, you can see that they had developed a very good system of self-preservation.

All the *Ceratopsians* had parrot beaks and special teeth. Most of the plant eaters we have studied had grinding teeth to crush up soft vegetable matter. The *Ceratopsians,* however, had cheek teeth that worked like big scissors. The teeth in the lower jaw fitted in between the teeth in the upper jaw, and sliced up the food. We can only conclude that the horned dinosaurs lived on rather tough, fibrous food, probably the fronds from cycad and palm trees. The slicing action was achieved by very strong jaw muscles, which in the case of *Triceratops* were over three feet long!

The easiest way to look at individual *Ceratopsians* is by numbers. That is, numbers of horns. *Protoceratops* had no horns as such, but a bony bump on his nose which might have had a sort of horn attached to it when he was alive. He was about six feet long and had a modest neck frill. Already his head made up nearly a third of his total length. We know from fossilized eggs and babies that when born he had hardly any neck frill and that this grew only as he got older.

Our next customer is *Monoclonius* (one stemmed) who had just one horn on the front of his face, rather like a modern rhinoceros. He grew to be sixteen feet long and had a bigger neck frill that had holes in it – perhaps to reduce its weight. He already shows clear signs of the thick muscles joining the neck frill to the shoulders. This arrangement must have limited the extent to which he could turn his head, and he must have relied on spearing his enemies by charging straight at them.

The biggest of the *Ceratopsian* dinosaurs was *Triceratops* (three horned). He grew to be over twenty feet long and had a deadly arrangement of horns, carrying one on his nose and one above each eye. Charging with his eight or nine tons of weight behind these horns, he must have been a formidable sight. A *Tyrannosaurus* impaled on these couldn't have lasted long.

As you can see from the photograph on this page, *Triceratops'* neck frill was a solid, saddle-shaped piece of bone with bony lumps at the edges. His whole skull, including frill and horns, was nearly as long as his body. Apart from its size and length, this skull had those great scissor-like teeth. These teeth were stacked one on top of the other, so that when one

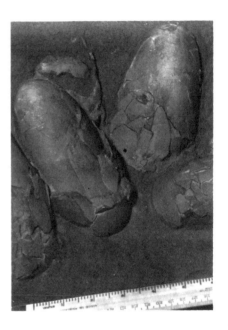

Top: **Triceratops** *skeleton.*
Above: **Protoceratops** *eggs.*

Above: **Protoceratops** *eggs hatching out. Notice the small neck at this age.*

Below: reconstructions of **Triceratops** *and* **Styracosaurus** *from their skeletons to show how they would have appeared in life. Opposite: a selection of the strange headed hadrosaurs in a typical setting. You can see the common feature of their duckbills and the differing shapes of their crests.*

TRICERATOPS

wore out, another took its place. They sliced away at the tough and stemmy plants and effectively reduced them to little pieces.

Although he was the biggest *Ceratopsian*, *Triceratops* was not the strangest-looking. At the foot of this page you will see *Styracosaurus* (spiny reptile), a three-and-a-half tonner. Instead of having horns pointing forwards, he had a neck frill with six sharp spikes, pointing backwards and outwards. On his nose he had one big thirty-inch horn. His head was really astonishing, being over seven feet long from neck frill to nose, and over five feet wide. His fossil skull looks rather like a hat rack, but alive he was more than a match for the meat eaters.

There are various other combinations of horns and neck frills, but these are some of the more exciting ones. Why there was such a variety, no one seems to know. We shall just have to add this riddle to all the others that exist in the story of the dinosaurs.

The Cretaceous period was remarkable for a number of new developments, but the peculiarity of its dinosaurs must be one of its most extraordinary features. In particular, this period seems to be rich in peculiar heads. From the fearsome horns and spikes of the horned dinosaurs, we move to the ridiculous-looking duckbilled dinosaurs.

STYRACOSAURUS

Duckbilled dinosaurs

This whole group is known as *Hadrosaurs* (big reptiles). They were not big by comparison with *Diplodocus* or *Brontosaurus,* but they were among the biggest *Ornithopods.* As a group they were very similar. They walked on two feet, and each foot had three rounded hoofs. Their arms were quite strong and ended in three fingers with little hoofs on them. They were mostly between thirty and forty feet long, and weighed about four tons. They all had duckbills with no teeth, but they had many cheek teeth.

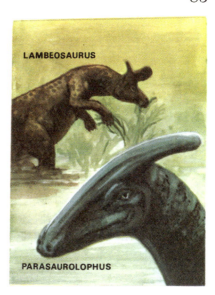

LAMBEOSAURUS

PARASAUROLOPHUS

CORYTHOSAURUS

ANATOSAURUS

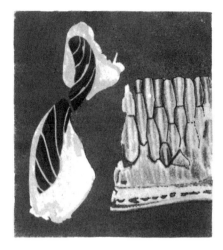

Above: illustration of the grinding action and "spare teeth" in the hadrosaurs.

Above: **Pachycephalosaurus,** *a strange ornithopod with a skull roof of solid bone.*

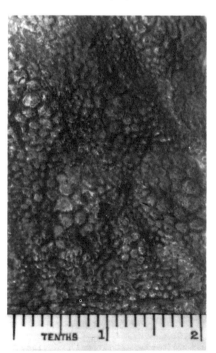

The *Hadrosaurs* are the animals that we referred to way back at the beginning of the book when we talked of "mummified skeletons". Some of the duck-billed dinosaurs obligingly died in the desert. There, in the fierce heat of the sun, their bodies dried out before they rotted. The wind soon covered them with sand and in time they fossilized, complete with skin and other tough parts. This has given us a superb opportunity to study what the outside *and* inside of a dinosaur looked like, for a change. If you look at the photograph below you can see for yourself how beautifully preserved these fossil skins were.

The mummified skeletons also give us some valuable information about these animals' hands and feet. Their fingers and toes were webbed, and they could certainly swim well, for their strong flattened tails were also like a crocodile's. They probably took to the water to escape the meat eaters who preyed on them. They had no horns or armour to defend themselves with, so flight was their only hope.

One of the mummified skeletons had its stomach intact, and the contents were pine needles, lots of different seeds and fruits and even some pieces of twig. So we know the *Hadrosaurs* didn't live on water plants or fish, but on tough land plants. This conclusion is supported by the teeth in this group of animals. They had the same system of "spare" teeth that we saw in some of the horned dinosaurs. Instead of the two sets of teeth working inside each other in a scissor action, the *Hadrosaur* teeth met at an angle to grind up fibrous food. The grinding surface of the teeth was coated with a hard enamel to avoid rapid wearing away. Since each side of the upper and lower jaw had something like two or three hundred teeth in it, the *Hadrosaur* was walking about with a mouth full of over a thousand teeth!

The oddest thing about the *Hadrosaurs* is the strange crests that some of them grew on their heads. These are not easy to describe, so look at page 85. *Hadrosaurus* himself, who gives his name to the group, had no crest at all. *Corythosaurus* had a crest such as you see on some old Greek helmets. *Lambeosaurus* looked as if he was wearing a hat several sizes too small for him, and *Parasaurolophus* had a crest rather like a swimmer's snorkel.

There have been lots of reasons suggested for these crests. The most likely is that they provided the animals with an acute sense of smell. If you had no horns or armour and simply had to run away from your enemies, it was invaluable to be able to tell when they were coming. Judging by their eye sockets, *Hadrosaurs* also had very keen eyesight, comparable to that of many modern birds.

These sharp-eyed *Hadrosaurs* with their peculiar heads were very common in the Upper Cretaceous. They had developed rapidly, but all to no avail. At the beginning of the next period there was nothing but fossilized skeletons to mark where they had been.

Tyrants with long teeth

Although the earlier *Allosaurs* and *Megalosaurs* were still around in the earlier part of the Cretaceous period, they were dwindling. The rulers on the land were now the *Deinodonts* (terror teeth). These were enormous and terrifying creatures. *Gorgosaurus* (terrible reptile) and *Tyrannosaurus* (tyrant reptile) are the most widely known of these huge predators.

Gorgosaurus, who was the first of the two to appear, was over thirty feet long. He walked on powerful legs which ended in huge bird-like feet. These feet were equipped with three long sharp claws. *Gorgosaurus* had a big skull with the typical carnivore's long, sharp teeth. Strangely enough, the very useful front limbs of the Jurassic *Allosaurs* had dwindled, and *Gorgosaurus* had only a puny pair of arms with three clawed fingers on the end.

The last of the predatory dinosaurs to appear was *Tyrannosaurus*. As far as we know, he was the biggest meat-eating animal ever to live on earth. At his maximum size he was fifty feet long and, in spite of his sloping posture, he was nearly twenty feet tall. He probably weighed about eight tons! This weight was supported on two enormously strong

Above: **Tyrannosaurus's** *skull, over 4 feet long and equipped with cruel razor-sharp teeth and a loose hinge to help swallowing.*

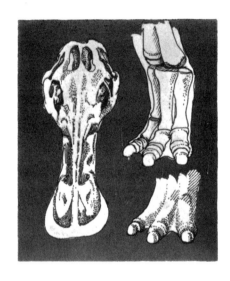

Above: the skull and skeleton foot of a hadrosaur, and the webbing of the toes.

Above: swimming hadrosaur, showing use of flat tail. Opposite: mummified skin of the hadrosaur **Trachodon**.

Above: the small front limbs of **Tyrannosaurus,** *whose use is something of a mystery to scientists.*

Above: **Gorgosaurus,** *one of the Cretaceous carnivores.*

Above: the foot of **Tyrannosaurus** *compared with a six foot man to show the scale of this great beast.*

legs, with equally large feet. His frightful two-clawed feet were thirty inches long and nearly as wide and he had a stride of nearly fourteen feet. His great skull was made in a rigid form, unlike *Allosaurus* whose skull was quite elastic at the joints. This enormous four-foot skull carried a set of six-inch dagger-like teeth with saw edges.

Tyrannosaurus' long, strong tail kept him nicely balanced as he went about the country attacking and eating many of the plant eaters that we have already seen. It is doubtful whether any of the other animals alive at the time could completely withstand the frightful effect of those feet and teeth in combination. A look at the illustrations of this terror of the Upper Cretaceous landscape will show you what the plant eaters had to contend with.

Strangely enough, not all the *Deinodonts* were the size of *Tyrannosaurus.* Some of them weighed only half a hundredweight and were no bigger than a large dog. They were no less fierce, however, and ate lizards and any other small animals that crossed their path, including some of the small mammals who were quietly growing and spreading in the shelter of the Cretaceous woodlands.

Meet your ancestors

In earlier periods we have seen mammal-like reptiles and then some true mammals. All the early mammals were small, with slender bones. These are easily fragmented and almost impossible to reassemble in their fossil form. Also, many of these mammals were eaten by carnivorous dinosaurs, who probably chewed them well!

There were descendants of the old *Pantotheres* in two forms. One group was animals with pouches – probably rather like our modern opossum. A second group consisted of animals who grew the young inside the mothers until they were fully formed. The Cretaceous version of these mammals were probably insect eaters, and may have looked like hedgehogs or shrews.

The new mammals on the scene were the multituberculates. Like the *Tritylodonts,* they looked somewhat like rats. They came in all sizes from two inches to two feet long. This group is of particular interest because they were plant-eating animals. Most of the other small mammals were meat eaters. From this selection of Cretaceous mammals all our present-day animals are descended.

Just so long as the dinosaurs ruled the earth, the mammals remained small and rather shy. Once the dinosaurs departed, there was a huge development of mammals and a great variety of forms appeared.

Reconstruction of **Ichthyornis,** *above, with* **Hesperornis** *in the background.*

Look up!

The Cretaceous relatives of the early flying reptiles grew bigger and even stranger to look at than their predecessors.

One of the early Cretaceous forms is *Dsungaripterus,* who lived in China. He was ten feet across the wings and had an odd-looking beak, which curved up in the same shape as an avocet's. He was a midget beside the later *Pteranodon* (winged, toothless). *Pteranodon* grew to twenty-five feet across the wings, but had a body the size of a turkey.

Pteranodon had developed a special sort of backbone that strengthened the joint between his spine and his wings. He had jaws like a pelican but no teeth and, at the back of his head, a long crest. This may have been necessary to balance his great jaws, or he may have used it to help him steer.

Reconstruction of **Hesperornis,** *above, the six foot powerful swimming bird of the Cretaceous seas.*

He lived on fish and must have been as terrifying in the air as some of the marine monsters were in the sea. Since he could not walk on his feet, it is also a puzzle to know how he rested and where. Perhaps he landed on cliff tops, and could launch himself like a glider. We shall never know, for before the end of the Cretaceous period he had gone. Perhaps his adaptation was just not good enough.

The birds that may have competed with *Pteranodon* are as infuriating as the Cretaceous mammals. They left very slight evidence in the form of fossils.

Such evidence as we do have indicates that there

Above: **Pteranodon,** *the Cretaceous pterosaur.*

Top: opossum and below, shrew, typical of the sort of mammals that lived in the Cretaceous undergrowth. They represent the pouched and insect eating animals. The fossil evidence they left is very fragmentary.

Above: multituberculates probably looked something like this. They were insect eaters and the ancestors of many present day mammals.

were several different types of bird at this time. Some were like herons, and others were like gulls.

Thanks to a vast Cretaceous sea in North America, there are two birds about which we have rather better knowledge. These are *Hesperornis* (bird of the west) and *Ichthyornis*. The former was essentially a sea bird, about four feet long. He had very powerful legs for swimming and diving, set well back on his body. There were disadvantages to this. *Hesperornis* could not walk on land because his weight was too far forward for him to balance. To add to his problems, his wings had dwindled until there was nothing left but a stick-like bone, so he couldn't fly either!

Side by side with *Hesperornis* was *Ichthyornis*. There was no doubt about *his* flying ability. His well-developed wings and breastbone make it clear that he was a powerful flyer. *Ichthyornis* also lived on fish. Like *Hesperornis*, he had the strong, clawed feet of his reptile ancestors. Both these birds seem to have lived in flocks, much as our modern sea birds do, but this didn't save them from extinction. Fortunately there were plenty of other birds to carry on the species into the later periods.

Giants in the water

The Cretaceous seas had more than their fair share of large reptiles. For a start, there were the two forms of *Plesiosaur*, the short-necked and the long-necked. The long-necked ones had small heads, and the short-necked ones large or long heads. They were very widely distributed all over the world.

A typical short-necked member of the group was *Kronosaurus*, who was about forty feet long. He swam strongly with his four flippers and his powerful tail. His ten foot skull was largely taken up by a long and very efficient jaw, full of short, sharp teeth. He ate a variety of marine creatures, and had the distinction of possessing the largest reptile skull ever known.

While *Kronosaurus* was busy developing his large skull, *Elasmosaurus* was growing a fantastically long neck. This accounted for a large part of his forty-seven-foot length. He appears to have used this very flexible neck to dart at prey. He could snatch both birds and *Pterosaurs* as they flew low over the water. Under the water, he could flick his cruel head into the middle of a shoal of fish before they had time to dart away. Although his head was comparatively small, it was armed with very sharp teeth.

In fierce competition with *Kronosaurus* and *Elasmosaurus* were the *Mosasaurs,* or sea lizards. They were related to the modern "Komodo Dragon". In the latter part of the Cretaceous period they were found in seas all over the world. Their adaptation from their lizard ancestors to a marine life was superb. Their limbs had become shorter and their toes webbed. This gave them four flippers, which they used in combination with their sculling tail. They had the special jaw hinge that we have seen in some of the carnivores. They sometimes grew to be fifty feet long, so you can imagine the terror they struck into most of the Cretaceous sea creatures. They came in various sizes and shapes, but they were all fierce and aggressive.

Among those who had reason to fear the *Mosasaurs* was a giant marine turtle called *Archelon.* His great body was twelve feet long and he had developed good, broad webbed flippers. To reduce his weight and give him better buoyancy, his shell had lost some of its bony parts and was reduced to a very functional minimum.

The Upper Cretaceous landscape was heavily populated with a wide variety of animal life. The *Stegosaurs, Pterosaurs, Ichthyosaurs* and the toothed birds which had been dwindling in numbers for some time were no longer present. There were herds of horned dinosaurs, some armoured dinosaurs, a few duck-billed dinosaurs and many of the *Theropods* still running about. Yet, as soon as we move into the Tertiary period they have all disappeared. Not a dinosaur fossil in sight. Suddenly all our subject matter has gone, and left us with nothing but a huge question – why?

Above: **Protoceratops** *eggs were laid in circles, like those of our modern turtle.*

Above: sauropod eggs, laid in smaller groups or singly had a capacity of nearly six pints.

Above: **Kronosaurus's** *skull, beside a figure which gives some idea of its huge size. The whole plesiosaur was over forty feet long and was found in Australia.*

Above: the komodo dragon, a modern close relative of the mosasaurs of the Cretaceous period. They all belong to the lizard family.

Tylosaurus, *above, was a 26 foot sea-going lizard. You can see his paddle-like fins and flat tail.*

This 12 foot sleek fish, above, was **Portheus**, *who provided food for many of the large marine reptiles.*

The big question mark

MANY people have delved into the question of why the dinosaurs and other prehistoric animals died out so suddenly. They have often come up with answers as varied as they were unlikely. First of all, let us see what the question is that we are trying to answer.

Did those early reptiles really die out so suddenly? It depends on what you mean by suddenly. There is probably a span of half a million years during which these animals dwindled and finally departed. Because it happened sixty or seventy million years ago our sense of time is distorted. We must also remember that a number of the animals we have studied had been diminishing for many millions of years. The disappearance was not so sudden, but still remarkable.

You have to dismiss the Biblical "Great Flood", Noah's Ark fashion, because this would not have selected just the dinosaurs for extinction. The same argument applies to disease, which is not likely to have affected so many different animals all over the world, and yet left others unscathed.

We are on slightly surer ground when we look at geographic and climatic theories. In Cretaceous times it was possible for animals to migrate over very wide areas of the world. Continents were not split up as they are now. This meant that the dinosaurs in different parts of the world were very similar. Something that adversely affected one would affect them all. The climate in Cretaceous times was similar in many parts of the world. The Tertiary period saw great changes in this respect. Many areas became noticeably cooler, and the variation in temperature in any one place was far greater. This was true both between night and day and between summer and winter.

PTERANODON

ELASMOSAURUS

TYLOSAURUS

Above: **Elasmosaurus** *and* **Pteranodon** *both hunting in the Cretaceous seas for fish and other sea creatures. Below: The vicious head of* **Tylosaurus** *competing with the other sea monsters for mastery of the sea.*

Large, cold-blooded animals do not like sharp changes in temperature, because of their lack of insulation. They can't adapt to them. The birds and mammals on the other hand can cope far better. They have a system of personal temperature control that will adjust to quite wide variations of air temperature.

Climatic and geographic changes would also affect vegetation, and therefore the diet of the plant eaters. If plant eaters die off, the diet of the carnivores that prey on them is suddenly cut off too. Some or all of these factors may have had a bearing on the disappearance of some of the most exciting creatures that have ever walked the earth.

In spite of all the evidence discussed in Chapter One, we are still mystified. The answer to "why did so many of the prehistoric animals become extinct so quickly?" eludes us and we must end this book on a big question mark.

Perhaps new evidence and new methods of investigation will eventually solve the riddle. Quite recently, fresh and previously unsuspected evidence of prehistoric life was found in Antarctica. The hunt is still on. Perhaps someone reading this book will be the one to come up with the answer.

Acknowledgements

Acknowledgement is due to the following for photographs (the number refers to the page on which the illustration appears). 29, 85 British Museum of Natural History. 49, 57, 89 Smithsonian Institute, Washington. 56-57 Princeton University. 68 Institut für Paläontologie und Museum der Humboldt-Universität, Berlin. 73 Institut und Museum für Geologie und Paläontologie der Universität, Tübingen. 89 Louis Thaler.